Explorations in Theology 9

Explorations in Theology 9

RONALD H.
PRESTON

SCM PRESS LTD

334 01981 8

First published 1981
by SCM Press Ltd
58 Bloomsbury Street, London WC1

Photoset by Input Typesetting Ltd
and printed in Great Britain by
Billing & Sons Ltd
London, Guildford and Worcester

164163

Contents

Introduction

Throughout my working life I have been under pressure from others to write and publish, but for a number of reasons I have not been in a position when it has been easy to respond. However, I am glad to be able to bring together in this book some material almost all of which has been previously published, but is not easily accessible. Limitations of space has meant a difficult problem of selection. The papers are printed in roughly chronological order and in substance are unchanged. One of the problems of writing in the field of social ethics is that the situations change so quickly that the illustrations make the writing seem out of date whether or not the underlying treatment is. That is one reason for excluding, apart from the first paper, anything written prior to 1970.

In the first I stray into the field of the New Testament specialist. We all have to take notice of what the biblical scholars are saying (a task laid upon us in addition to our own field of theological study), but to write in that field is perhaps too bold. My own view is that the paper, although presupposing a critical study of the gospels, is relatively independent of the more recent developments in that study; for instance redaction criticism, of which I know more now than I did in 1966. I think also it deals with a question of perennial importance. But I may be wrong; others will judge.

The second paper is one of several in this book concerned with ecumenical social ethics. One section has been omitted because it was solely concerned with the structure of the symposium to which the whole chapter formed an introduction. The rest in my judgment is still relevant to the method of studying issues in Christian social ethics in the ecumenical movement and to its conference procedures, as the recent one at the Massachusetts Institute of Technology showed (see the eighth paper).

The subject of the third paper, middle axioms, is one on which little has been written, and I have been asked on several occasions for copies of it. It needs expansion, partly to meet three criticisms. The first is that the method is elitist as compared with grass-roots participation. The previous paper deals implicitly, but only partially with this point. To answer it fully would require a treatment of both political and liberation theology, which I have in a form needing revision, and which I hope to publish in due course. The second criticism is that the method cannot work because ideological differences in modern society so influence thought as to make agreement on middle axioms impossible. This possibility has always been allowed for; that both because of ideological and other differences agreement at this middle level cannot be arrived at. But those who thought about middle axioms were well aware of ideologies, and of the study of the sociology of knowledge which alerts us to them. I myself have been familiar with these considerations since my undergraduate days. Those who think that humanity is so shut up in separate ideological groups that no common understanding is possible between them are in effect adopting a Marxist view in a particularly sharp and allegedly 'scientific' form which they need to justify. I do not think it can be justified on 'scientific' grounds; and there is of course a vast amount in the Christian tradition which would deny it, the Natural Law tradition in *any* form, Lutheran civic righteousness and Calvinist common grace among others. However, this is too large a subject to pursue further in this introduction. The third criticism is that it presupposes too static a view of Christian doctrine from which one starts, whereas there is a reciprocal relation between our understanding of the Christian faith we have received and our understanding of the world in the midst of which we are seeking to understand what we have received. Too static an impression of Christian doctrine may have been given by some exponents of the method of middle axioms, perhaps I have done so, but it is not essential to the position; and Reinhold Niebuhr, to quote one who approved of it, is certainly not open to this criticism.

Manchester University does not have the custom of Professorial Inaugural Lectures. Nevertheless, the student Theological Society asked me to explain myself in my first session as Professor, and the fourth paper represents a shortened version of my attempt to do so to a mainly undergraduate audience.

The Rylands Lecture, which constitutes the fifth paper, is self-explanatory. A further lecture, 'The Question of a Just, Participatory and Sustainable Society' appeared in the *Bulletin of the John Rylands Library*, Autumn 1980 and, like other Rylands lectures, is available in a separate booklet. It is particularly concerned with the recent MIT Conference of the WCC.

1981 is the centenary of the birth of William Temple, so it is appropriate to reprint in that year my introduction to the reissue of his *Christianity and Social Order*, a book which has still not lost its relevance.

The seventh paper was written for an issue of *Crucible*, the journal of the Board of Social Responsibility of the Church of England, which was specially designed with the 1978 meeting of the Lambeth Conference of Bishops of the Anglican Communion in mind, and was circulated to them all.

The eighth paper is the transcription of a BBC Radio Three talk. I have included it because for the three months after it was delivered, and repeated, I was receiving requests for copies, and for permission to circulate it in various groups and areas. I agreed in every case, but it made me decide that perhaps it should appear in print.

The ninth and eleventh papers are examples of brief working papers which I think may not have dated so much as to lose their interest; and again there is an ecumenical reference. The first was written for one of the Commissions of an International Consultation sponsored by the Irish School of Ecumenics in 1978. The plenary papers were subsequently published by the ISE with the title *Understanding Human Rights*. The eleventh paper was written for a symposium organized by UNIAPAC (an international body of Christian Business Executives whose headquarters is in Brussels), and was designed to answer specific questions put to churches by Christian executives in Transnational Companies who were disposed to think criticisms by the churches of such companies were unfair, and suspected the bases on which they were uttered.

The tenth paper is a review article. It was presumably because of this book that Dr Norman was invited to give the Reith Lectures of 1978 on 'Christianity and the World Order'. Their point of view is the same. I was tempted to include an unpublished detailed analysis and critique of the Reith Lectures, but

decided to reprint the review instead, because it deals with a
weighty book which will last, whilst the Reith Lectures by comparison are slight and ephemeral.

The last paper, originally published in Australia, is ostensibly
a risky exercise in looking ahead; but the effort to do so inevitably involves some estimate of the recent past, which is in fact
its predominant subject.

A bibliography of published work (but including only a few
reviews) is added to the book to assist readers who are interested in tracing any of them, sometimes in obscure places; it
goes back to a young man's efforts. In the years 1935–38 and
1943–48 most of my written work consisted of Study Outlines
for the Student Christian Movement of which I was Industrial
Secretary in the first period and Study Secretary in the second,
when I also edited and wrote for *The Student Movement*
magazine.

Manchester, Christmas Eve 1980   Ronald Preston

1

Ethical Criticisms of Jesus

The title is ambiguous. It could refer to ethical criticism made by Jesus of others, or it could refer to ethical criticisms made by others of Jesus. It is this latter which is our concern. The ambiguity could have been avoided by a title like 'Atheistic criticisms of Jesus', but that would not quite have served the purpose; for our interest is not in whether ethical criticisms which have been made of Jesus have come from atheists or not. They may also have come from adherents of other religions; or they may have come from Christians who are worried by some elements in the gospels which appear to accord ill with other elements in them, elements which seem of basic importance to the Christian faith. Our concern is with ethical criticisms made of Jesus from whatever source.

Such criticism is of peculiar importance to anyone who is a Christian. There are many objections to the Christian faith in the modern world. Some arise from doubts as to the whole possibility of meaningful speech about God, and require a revitalized natural theology to meet them. Some arise from historical doubts about the authenticity of the gospel narratives, and these require answering with all the resources of critical investigation which are now open to us. But even if these two sources of objection are dealt with, as indeed there is good reason to believe they can be,[1] a further one presents itself. This is the raising of ethical objections to Jesus.

The whole Jewish-Christian tradition has firmly linked moral goodness with an understanding of God's nature, and the Christian tradition has seen in Jesus Christ a decisive refining of that understanding as it had been inherited from the Old Testament. It has found the clue to the conflicts between Jesus

and the religious leaders of Judaism in a moral challenge to
recognize in his ministry a more radical goodness of God than
they had hitherto understood. It was a goodness which challenged their goodness and declared it inadequate. It was a
goodness which went out to seek and save the lost instead of
taking refuge in devoted study of the Torah and being careful
of the company it kept. It was a goodness which was so far-
reaching that the more you understood of it the more there was
yet to grasp, so that any thought of exhausting it by even the
most loving obedience to the details of Torah was beside the
point. It was a goodness which has been realized only once in
history, and by the man who lived what he taught. Christians
see in Jesus the divine goodness visibly earthed in human life,
and they have expressed this conviction in the doctrine of the
sinlessness of Jesus.

If, therefore, there are ethical attacks on Jesus, it is a challenge
to the heart of the Christian faith. Accordingly we propose to
give some indication of the orthodox Christian witness that
Jesus is the Perfect Man, and then mention some of the moral
attacks that have been made on him from time to time, before
dealing more fully with two more recent attacks on his ethical
teaching and the Christian life which follows from it.

I

The traditional Christian claim about the sinlessness of Jesus
arises out of the apostolic testimony about him. At least five
passages of scripture are of major importance in this connection,
which we will mention in what is probably their chronological
order:

1. 'For our sake he made him to be sin, who knew no sin, so
that in him we might become the righteousness of God' (II Cor.
5.21). This verse, with which Rom. 8.3 may be compared, presents considerable difficulties of exegesis from the point of view
of a doctrine of the atonement, the complexities of which are
not our concern now. But it seems clear that the phrase translated 'knew no sin' means 'practised no sin', the sufferings
which Jesus met with being due not to his own sins but those
of others.

2. 'For we have not a high priest who is unable to sympathize
with our weaknesses, but one who in every respect has been

tempted as we are, yet without sinning' (Heb. 4.15). This clearly asserts that Jesus could have sinned (for he was tempted to sin) but did not.

3. 'He committed no sin; no guile was found on his lips' (I Peter 2.22). This is a similar claim to the previous one.

4. 'You know that he appeared to take away sins, and in him there is no sin' (I John 3.5).

5. With this may be compared the question Jesus asks in John 8.46. 'Which of you convicts me of sin?', clearly implying 'no one can'. We are, of course, not taking this last as the literal words of Jesus, but as the result of reflection on the apostolic witness about Jesus (probably including the traditions about him preserved in the synoptic gospels). From his meditations on these the author of the Fourth Gospel has constructed his text.

The implications of this witness are that in Jesus the moral goodness of God himself was realized to the fullest possible extent in a life of a human being. More is being claimed than was claimed, for instance, by John Wesley who said of Fletcher of Madeley, 'I never heard him speak an improper word', and of whom his biographer said, 'He was without perceptible spot or flaw.' It is not, however, necessary to the claim to maintain that Jesus was free from original sin (however one may interpret this), or that he could not have been tempted. Many of the Fathers claimed this because of their belief in the Virgin Birth and their assumption that genetical inheritance came only from the father; now we know it comes equally from the mother (presumably the doctrine of the immaculate conception in the Roman Catholic Church is an attempt to deal with this).[2] The Fathers, however, were not much concerned about these questions; it was the divinity of Christ which exercised them and they tended to assume without much discussion that he lived a morally perfect life. It is perhaps worth remarking that such a belief implies a remarkable tribute to our Lord's family in the formative years of his upbringing for which we should do well to honour St Mary and Joseph.

What evidence is there in the synoptic gospels to justify the apostolic witness to the sinlessness of Jesus? Some of this witness dates from after the composition of these gospels, but some of it is before them, notably that of St Paul. It is, of course, impossible to prove a negative, that Jesus never sinned. Further we have only a little access into Jesus' inward motives. But making all necessary reservations of this kind, it is noteworthy that in the gospels Jesus shows no consciousness of sin, even of forgiven sin, and no scars from past sins (such as we find in St Paul). Yet Jesus is precisely the one who produces a sense of sin in others, even those whom we would consider the most saintly of men. We find in the gospels a unity of character and a depth of goodness which it would be impossible to invent, for, as Rousseau remarked, an inventor of this would be greater than the subject he invented.

This is not because the gospels produce an artificially smooth impression. At least two incidents are left, firmly embodied in the oral traditions about Jesus, which clearly caused difficulty in view of the belief in the sinlessness of Jesus. The first is Jesus' baptism by John the Baptist, which appears to have crystallized his dawning sense of messianic vocation. We do not find any fundamental difficulty in reconciling this incident with the belief in Jesus' sinlessness, but Matthew seems to have felt a difficulty and to have dealt with it by verses 14 and 15 of chapter 3; but his sentence 'let it be so now; for thus it is fitting for us to fulfil all righteousness' has caused as much, if not more, trouble than the difficulty it was meant to elucidate.

The other difficulty is Jesus' answer to the rich young ruler in Mark 10.18: 'Why do you call me good? No one is good but God alone.' Matthew is again conscious of the difficulty and tones down Jesus' answer (19.17) to 'Why do you ask me about what is good?' Again there is no fundamental difficulty, as the author of John's gospel has seen in his meditations. God alone is absolute goodness; the goodness of Jesus is the result of moral growth gained through temptation and trial. 'Not I, but my Father in me' is the recurring theme of the Fourth Gospel. 'The Son can do nothing of his own accord, but only what he sees the Father doing' (John 5.19). This is spelled out more fully in the epistle to the Hebrews: 'Although he was a Son, he learned obedience through what he suffered; and being made perfect he became the source of eternal salvation to all who obey him' (5.8f.). The road of obedience led from the temptations to the garden of Gethsemane, and all the way Jesus made a complete response until the full extent of his messianic vocation was accomplished. 'It is finished' is the last word from the cross in St John's passion narrative.

The witness of the synoptic gospels and the apostolic testimony agree. Rough hewn as it is, and obviously feeling its way in putting into words its convictions about the moral goodness of Jesus, it is all the more impressive that it could do no other than respond to the goodness it had found in Jesus by claiming that he was without sin. The Christian tradition could do no other than maintain this claim. All the more important, therefore, is it that ethical criticisms made of Jesus should be taken seriously.

II

Some ethical criticisms made of Jesus arise from a misunderstanding of Jesus' messianic vocation and of the eschatological urgency of the coming of the kingdom or rule of God which is the key to the deeds and words of his ministry. These matters are all dealt with in standard commentaries and expositions and there is no point in going into the details of them here. It will suffice merely to mention some of them. The parable of the unjust steward (Luke 16.1) is not meant to commend sharp practice; the saying 'let the dead bury their dead . . .' in Matt. 8.22 is not a slur on the family; the cursing of the fig tree (Mark 11.13) and the cleansing of the temple (Mark 11.15) are not exhibitions of petulance; the saying to the Syro-Phoenician woman (Mark 7.27) is not a slur on Gentiles but a reference to the messianic days in Israel preceding the ingathering of the Gentiles.

A little more should be said about two more serious criticisms which often puzzle Christians as well as non-Christians. The first concerns Jesus' attitude to the Rabbis. C. G. Montefiore says 'What one would have wished to find would be one single incident in which Jesus actually performed one loving deed to one of his Rabbinic antagonists or enemies,'[3] and he adds that an ounce of practice would be worth a ton of theory. On this there are three things to be said. The first is that there are hints in the gospels that there were better relationships between Jesus and the Pharisees than is obvious to the casual reader. (See Mark 12.34; Luke 7.36 and 13.31.) The second is that the gospels as we now have them reflect the split which soon arose between the church and the synagogue in the early days of Christianity. At first the Christians were all devout Jews who attended the synagogue (and in Jerusalem the temple) and who differed from their fellow-Jews only in believing that the Messiah had come

But before long Gentiles outnumbered Jews in the church and, what was especially provoking to the Jews, the church attracted the 'god-fearers' from the Gentile world. These were people who were attracted by the lofty monotheism of Judaism and its high morality but who, because of circumcision and the food laws, could not bring themselves actually to become Jews although they were adherents of the synagogue. In Christianity they found a faith with all the depth of Judaism and more, but without its ritualistic disadvantages. After the fall of Jerusalem in AD 70 feeling between Christians and Jews got worse. Christians interpreted this catastrophe as a divine judgment on Judaism and one that Jesus had foretold. It is impossible to study passages like Matthew 23 without paying attention to these factors, which have undoubtedly influenced their transmission in the church.

But the third thing that needs to be said is that there was a root issue between Jesus and the Pharisees which could not help but be focussed sharply. Jesus' whole ministry was, as we have seen, a demand for moral insight. The Pharisees could not grasp this because they were blinded by their own goodness, and pleased with it. It was not their bad points which blinded them but their good ones. A more radical goodness was attacking them at their strong point and this was far more upsetting to their pride than to have their weaknesses pointed out. This they might well have accepted. But in showing that their understanding of divine goodness was not radical enough, indeed that – good as it was – it was wrongly based and therefore needed a root and fundamental change, it was impossible that Jesus could avoid a fundamental conflict with the Pharisees.

The other common criticism, found among Christians and non-Christians alike, is the extent to which Jesus appears to emphasize rewards and punishments (the hope of heaven and the fear of hell) as motives for conduct, instead of commending right conduct for its own sake. The most difficult passage about rewards is found in Luke 14.7, the story of the guests at the marriage feast, which appears to appeal to enlightened self-interest of the 'honesty is the best policy' type in precisely the same way that so much of the ethics of the wisdom literature does. This passage is unique in the gospels and in view of this we are entitled to try and interpret it in the light of the rest. What seems likely is that in the oral tradition the original setting of this teaching has been lost and Luke's explanation of it is not the right one. (He has a similar difficulty with the parable of the unjust steward, as can be seen by the incongruous verses tacked on to the end of it. Luke 16.1–12.) Jesus' parables bring home the radical nature of the kingdom of God, as he understood it, by illustrations drawn from everyday life. Sometimes they are by contrast as, for instance, the parable of the labourers in the vineyard (Matt. 20.1–16), which shews that reckoning in the kingdom of God is topsy turvy by everyday standards. Sometimes they are on the *a fortiori* principle: if something is characteristic of human life, how much more is it the case in the kingdom of God. In these latter parables Jesus often takes examples of worldly conduct (as in the case of the unjust steward) to bring out his meaning more forcefully. In this case he is saying that if common manners and etiquette suggest a certain modesty of behaviour at a wedding breakfast, how much more is egoism out of place in the kingdom of God.

The general characteristic of Jesus' ethical teaching is to link it on the one hand with what God has already done and is doing for mankind and on the other with life after death. The first is the main and most distinctive motive. 'You have received without pay, give without pay' (Matt. 10.8) is its keynote. God's signal graciousness to men is shewed in nature, his vital benefits of sunshine and rain being bestowed on all irrespective of merit; it is shewn in human life in the gracious ministry of Jesus. Blessings precede obedience. Obedience arises from a life of grateful response to God for the blessings. On the other hand it is true that much of the teaching also looks to an eternal reward, but the motivation involved is much misunderstood. It states what must be the case if God be indeed the God and Father of our Lord Jesus Christ. Christ-like conduct must bring the doer into the presence of God. The pure in heart will see God. That is their reward; but it is only a reward for those who follow Jesus for love's sake, not the reward's sake. Indeed in the latter case they would not appreciate it if they got it. God cannot be loved by highminded but self-centred people.

Jesus' teaching on punishment is equally vivid. There is his illustration in Mark 9.48ff. of Gehenna, the perpetually burning rubbish dump outside Jerusalem, destroying the city's refuse by fire; there is his allegory of the sheep and the goats in Matthew 25. Clearly Jesus believed in the possibility of spiritual ruin and destruction. His most pessimistic saying is his contrast between the broad and narrow ways in Matt. 7.13f. This must

be balanced against parables such as the prodigal son which
suggest that God will never give up those who do not want to
give him up, no matter how wayward they are. Whether anyone
will bring himself to spiritual destruction we cannot know. We
certainly cannot dismiss the possibility in our own case. The
New Testament does not give one clear answer to this. There
are on the other side hints that all will be saved, for instance in
Rom. 11.32, but we shall be wise not to presume upon them,
and there seems no ground for criticizing Jesus for stating what
is a clear possibility. But we must not attribute to him ideas of
eternal punishment which he did not hold and which have been
fathered on him in later ages. The root point is that neither a
morality of fear nor one based on a selfish pursuit of rewards
can produce purity of heart, and that references to both rewards
and punishments in the teaching of Jesus must be interpreted
in the light of his vital and central call for obedient love as the
only appropriate response to the graciousness of God. Once
this is grasped there is not much difficulty in shewing that it is
abundant life that Jesus intends for us, and that the self-sacrifice
involved is not a cramping thing but a fulfilment. What it demands that we should give up is a perverse attempt to hug to
ourselves alone blessings which can only be won in a mutual
fellowship and exchange of love.

III

When we turn to explicitly atheistic criticisms of Jesus the mind
tends to go back to the nineteenth-century figure of Nietzsche,
the son of a German Lutheran pastor. Influenced by the new
knowledge of evolution, he extrapolated the concept from the
biological sphere and applied it to the social process. He
preached the morality of power, in view of the death of God,
and regarded the stress on Jesus and his cross as a corrupting
influence, a Jewish plot, to take revenge upon the master people
of the world: This thinking had a good deal of influence in Nazi
Germany, and writers in the 1930s had to deal with him. But
fortunately that period has passed. He may come to the fore
again, but at the moment we need not dwell any further on
him.

One would expect radical criticisms of Jesus from Marxist
sources in view of its avowed atheistic basis and its hostility to
all religion. There is, in fact, very little. This is largely because

Marxist writers are apt to regard Jesus as a legend. Marx's only comment on Jesus is alleged to be that he liked his attitude to children. Engels paid much more attention to him, and other Marxist writers have tended to follow his line of thought. He regarded Revelation as the earliest book in the New Testament. This, he thought, gives a mythical picture of Jesus, and it was in the second century that the gospels were written, fiction in the guise of history, to provide the features of an historical person. Lenin adopted the Christ-myth theory of Arthur Drews, which was popular at the turn of the century. It was often repeated in popular booklets published by the former Rationalist Press Association. The theory is completely discredited, and the booklets no longer appear on the bookstalls. But it is still likely to be found in Communist school textbooks, for instance in East Germany, which hover between bald summaries of Jesus' life and assertions that he is a mythical figure.[4] There are few disrespectful words about him, rather a refusal to take him seriously. Another reason for this is that historical materialism holds the masses to be the creators of history and refuses to admit the importance of a single person. Marxist writings, then, contain much criticism of the church and of the social role of religion, but little of Jesus.

A different kind of atheistical attack on Jesus is found in Richard Robinson's *An Atheist's Values*.[5] In the course of his book, which has many valuable things to say, Robinson devotes a section to a criticism of Jesus' ethical teaching which deserves careful thought. His first criticism is one we have met before. It concerns the prominent strain of harshness in it. There is little of Matthew Arnold's 'sweet reasonableness'. There is much about weeping and gnashing of teeth. There is the saying about shaking the dust off one's feet against the indifferent (Mark 6.11); there is the sin against the Holy Ghost (Mark 3.29); there is the upbraiding of Chorazin and Bethsaida (Matt. 11.20); there is Jesus' offhand attitude to his family (Matt. 12.46), and his expectation of parricide as a result of his mission (Matt. 10.21). All these arise out of the eschatological rigour, to which we have already referred; a study of them in any commentary would shew that the sharpness in them is not sinister but a way of bringing home the radical nature of the challenge to a new and deeper moral insight.

Robinson goes on to summarize the ethical teaching of Jesus in five points, on each of which he comments. (*i*) *Love God,*

which means repent and be righteous. This involves improvidence and, as a substitute for thrift and prudence, prayer and
faith. (*ii*) *Believe in me*. We should reject both these demands,
and the improvidence which goes with them, because they are
made without reference to probability. (*iii*) *Love man*, which will
mean non-resistance, forgiveness and generosity. The improvidence recommended by the first demand will impede the ful-
filling of this third one. We should accept this command with
the proviso that it overstates the forgiveness of, and non-resistance to, bullies; we should also remember that in the gospels
it is overshadowed by the harsh and unloving behaviour of the
preacher and by its absolute subordination to the first two commands.[6] (*iv*) *Be pure in heart*. This is wise if it warns against
dangerous emotions and desires, but it goes too far if it rules
out contemplation by the imagination of evil in life and in art.
(*v*) *Be humble*. This means respect rather than contempt for
others, with no censoriousness or displays of superiority. This
is right, but humility must not over-ride the importance of
having a *true* estimate of oneself and of others.

Robinson then complains of the absence in Jesus' teaching of
the three Greek virtues of *beauty* (except a reference to lilies to
teach improvidence), *truth* (for Jesus demands faith by which
he means 'believing certain very improbable things without
considering evidence or estimating probabilities; and that is
contrary to reason' – p. 149), and *justice*. Jesus is silent about a
vast number of important ethical questions.

> Jesus says nothing on any social question except divorce, and all
> ascriptions of any political doctrine to him are false. He does not
> pronounce about war, capital punishment, gambling, justice, the
> administration of law, the distribution of goods, socialism, equality
> of income, equality of sex, equality of colour, equality of oppor-
> tunity, tyranny, freedom, slavery, self-determination, or contracep-
> tion. There is nothing Christian about being for any of these things,
> nor about being against them, if we mean by 'Christian' what Jesus
> taught according to the Synoptic Gospels (p. 149).

Robinson concludes this section of his book with the words,

> The reasons Jesus gave for his precepts, namely his promises and
> threats, are quite unacceptable. They are false, since there is no
> heaven or hell; and anyhow they make his precepts precepts of
> prudence instead of precepts of morality. To obey rules because
> otherwise you will go to hell is prudence, not morality (p. 154).

Some of these points have been dealt with in our previous

discussion. Some of them derive from a disbelief in God and therefore in Jesus as the Christ of God, which is not our concern here. If one does believe in God these ethical criticisms fall to the ground. But whether there are sufficient grounds for such a belief or not are prior questions requiring quite separate treatment.

Robinson's point about beauty hardly holds. Apart from the question of the lilies, there is much beauty in the parables (indeed as an art form they are unique in the world's literature). Moreover beauty is involved in the whole doctrine of the incarnation, for the visions of God in the Bible (as Jesus well knew from his meditations on the Old Testament) are in terms of brightness, glory and beauty. It is precisely this glory which the New Testament writers find reflected in Jesus (Heb. 1.3). Robinson's point, however, is effective against some forms of Christianity which have shunned the beautiful and almost made a cult of the ugly.[7] His point about truth, however, involves a complete misunderstanding of what Jesus meant by faith. We have seen that it had nothing to do with blind faith but with moral discernment. 'And why do you not judge for yourselves what is right?' asks our Lord (Luke 12.57). It is possible that he added 'with all thy mind' to the summary of the law (Mark 12.30; Luke 10.27).[8] St Paul certainly understood the renewal of the mind to be involved in the Christian life (Rom. 12.2) and, as he shews in other matters, he is likely to have understood our Lord correctly.

There is, however, an important point arising out of Robinson's discussion of Jesus' demand for faith. The Bible has no place for 'honest doubt'. It equates unbelief with sin. St Paul's reference in II Cor. 4.4 to 'unbelieving minds blinded by the god of this world' is typical. This may be so, but the question is whether the blindness is always culpable; how far it is vincible or invincible, to borrow two terms from moral theology. In Jesus' day everyone believed in God. The question was, *what* God? Jesus was making a demand for moral insight to recognize a radical goodness and to see in it a revelation of God himself. Today millions do not believe in God. True, much of the disbelief is undoubtedly dishonest doubt which recalls Kierkegaard's saying that 'it is hard to believe because it is hard to obey'. But we have reached a new position in human affairs, having its roots in the scientific revolution of the seventeenth century, where many honestly cannot believe in God. This is an entirely different position for Christian theology compared with most of its history or with New Testament times. Theology today must leave room for doubt. Faith must leave room for unfaith and indeed learn from it; both must want the truth above all else.

Robinson's remaining point is his listing of all the issues Jesus does not deal with, culminating in the charge of a lack of concern for justice. Here the point surely is that Jesus concentrated on the one, decisive, central issue of his messianic mission. This was to vindicate the highly paradoxical Rule of God in the world, so topsy turvy by everyday standards. By word and deed he strove to jolt his Jewish contemporaries to recognize in his ministry the radical goodness of God. He deliberately did not deal with the relative issues of his own day. He refused to divide an inheritance between brothers (Luke 12.13f.). He refused to say which obligations are due to the state, but laid down the basic principle that some are (Mark 12.17). The sayings about divorce seem the only exception that can be made to this characteristic of his teaching, but it is questionable whether they are. The basic passage, Mark 10.1–12, need not be interpreted as a rule for the church but as a fundamental statement of the nature of marriage, and the famous Matthean exception about divorce[9] raises acutely whether Matthew has preserved the oral tradition without an intrusive element related to current Rabbinic controversies. It is more plausible to interpret the teaching on divorce on the same lines as the rest of Jesus' ethical teaching, and to say that he deliberately did not deal with relative issues of his day. His task was to set our feet upon the way of goodness as citizens of the kingdom of God, a way which is inexhaustible. We may be thankful he did not go further into details or we should have the same trouble with the gospels that the Muslims have with the Koran in relating details of a past age to a quite different situation today. We have to bring Jesus' radical ethic to bear on the problems of our day, and we have at least one good example in the New Testament of how in the early church a Christian did precisely this. He is St Paul. We have his general ethical teaching (in which he has got to the heart of our Lord's teaching), and his application of it to current problems.[10] Down the centuries the Christian church has tried to discharge this same task with varying success. There is much to criticize at times. Submissiveness, for instance, has been overstressed in Christian teaching, particularly to the underprivileged. The church needed to learn that it is precisely in the concern for justice that Christian love finds its appropriate expression for the collective relationships of men, but she has followed this insight only fitfully, and in this respect could fairly be the subject of the strictures by Robinson.

IV

We have grown accustomed since the time of the Victorian agnostics like T. H. Huxley, to people who regarded the Christian faith as outworn and incredible but accepted the Christian way of life as right. In some respects Professor P. H. Nowell-Smith of the University of Kent is a successor to these. In a broadcast discussion with Mr J. Lucas early in 1963 on 'Christian Morals'[11] he stated that he had no disagreement with the content of Christian ethics. He favoured love rather than malice, sympathy rather than callousness, loyalty rather than treachery. It is the form of the ethics he objected to. The basis of ethics can be deontological, in which case moral rules are like orders and their validity depends on their source. This leads to the acceptance of these rules not because we see the point of them but because they are commanded, in this case by God. (The fact that he may command them from benevolent motives is irrelevant.) On the other hand the basis of ethics can be teleological, in which case moral rules look towards some end, and we can assess them, in the light of experience, by their consequences. They are rather like, for example, the rules of skill in card games like whist, where experience shews that the maximum is made of whatever hand is dealt if the rule 'second player plays low, third player plays high' is followed, or in bridge the rule that in relation to the dummy one leads through strength and up to weakness. Nowell-Smith pointed out that there are teleological elements in Christian ethics, and he singled out our Lord's saying 'the sabbath was made for man, not man for the sabbath' (Mark 2.27), but they are mixed with a large deontological element of which he disapproves. This involves a one-sided dependence of an impotent creature on an omnipotent Creator. The human analogy is that of a father to a very young child.

He appealed for support to the work of the Swiss educational psychologist, Piaget. Investigating the growth of moral ideas in children, Piaget illustrated the matter from playing with marbles. If you give a very young child marbles he will just throw them around; there is no game. From the ages of about five to nine there is a game and there are rules; these may be laid down by parents or by older children, and are taken very seriously. Children learn what is wrong before they know *why* it is wrong. They may be punished if they infringe the rule, but whether they are or not what is wrong is what is forbidden. From about the age of ten children begin to ask questions about the rules; they realize that they depend on mutual consent and that they can be adapted in the light of the various purposes for which they have been formulated. From this work of Piaget's it would appear that Christian ethics is appropriate to the mental ages of five to nine but that it tends to fix the believer in an immature attitude, a reluctance to grow up and to pass from dependence to freedom and maturity, and hence to responsibility.[12]

Nowell-Smith is right to support a teleological element in ethics and to find an element of it in the teaching of Jesus. The trouble with his view is that it is too atomistic and that it overlooks the Christian doctrine of conscience. According to this the Christian faith must be freely accepted and we cannot be right with God against our will. Certainly we must take steps to have an informed conscience, one not blinded by prejudice. But such as it is we must follow at any particular moment what our conscience dictates both in matters of faith and conduct. But this autonomy of the conscience is set in a heteronomous framework. We are meant to be committed to and in fellowship with one another in the bundle of life. We must therefore commit ourselves to someone else beyond the bounds of our knowledge if we have good grounds for doing so. This is, for instance, the proper basis of marriage. Lack of commitment to follow the path of marriage, come what may, 'for better for worse, for richer for poorer, in sickness and in health' is what causes so many marriages to go wrong. A half-commitment, a lurking idea that we can always get out of it if it does not come up to expectations, vitiates the whole undertaking from the start. Provided we have good grounds for embarking on a marriage it is right and necessary that we should commit ourselves beyond what we can know or foretell, and that our wills should abandon their autonomy and accept a heteronomous relationship. This is in no way an easy continuation of childlike obedience to parents. In the life of Jesus the deepest example of this is not connected with marriage but with his final dedication of himself to complete his Father's purposes through his own messianic vocation, even though it would lead him to Calvary. 'Not what I will, but what thou wilt' (Mark 14.36). Christians find this one of the deepest moments of divine self-revelation. Professor Nowell-Smith dislikes it.

Whether it is reasonable or not for us to trust in Christ depends on a prior question of Christian doctrine which is not our concern now. Professor Nowell-Smith is an atheist and so to him it cannot be reasonable. But if one does accept that Jesus Christ is God's saving word to men then it is quite reasonable to follow Christ's ethics. There is a necessary deontological basis to it, and also a teleological element in working it out in relation to particular issues. To do this is to grow into spiritual maturity, to grow towards 'the measure of the stature of the fullness of Christ' (Eph. 4.13). It is more than can be accomplished in a lifetime, for the further we go on this road the greater will be the perspectives opening up before us. In this process moral rules will have the useful place Nowell-Smith assigns to them, but will be subordinate to a goodness which is greater than the rules and demands a necessary flexibility in them.

To trust in Christ in this way builds up moral independence rather than fixing the believer in immature and childish attitudes. And this is exactly how good parents try to help the moral growth of their children, so that they will become morally independent of them whilst deeply attached at an adult level to a goodness which transcends them both. In our relation to Jesus Christ St Paul hits off the situation exactly when he says to the Galatians, 'For freedom Christ has set us free, stand fast therefore, and do not submit again to a yoke of slavery' (5.1).

V

There are relatively few ethical attacks on Jesus. It is the church which is usually, and often rightly, the target. Such attacks on Jesus as there are frequently rest on misunderstandings. Too often people do not come face to face with him. This may be because of this ethical criticism of the church, or because they have acquired erroneous impressions of Christian doctrine, or because of honest or dishonest doubts. The Christian must try to remove obstacles to belief on all these fronts, his aim being to help our generation to meet Jesus in his words and deeds and to enter into that understanding of God's gracious purposes for mankind which led him to his death on a cross. There the full challenge of the radical goodness of Jesus meets us, and we are compelled to weigh up for ourselves whether it is of God or of men, and whether in the end we can sustain a moral criticism of it or whether we do not find it criticizing us.

We have seen that Christian theology will have to take a new attitude to honest doubt, to the atheism and agnosticism which is a relatively new feature of the world's history. The doubt has arisen from the intellectual revolution and the rapid social changes brought about through the development of science and technology (which are themselves products of the one civilization deeply influenced by Christianity). We may venture a suggestion that this is a hazard which God has chosen for us as part of his liberation of man in Christ; it is something with which we must live and from aspects of which we must learn.

2

A Breakthrough in Ecumenical Social Ethics?

There is a widespread agreement that the years 1966–68 saw a breakthrough in ecumenical social ethics. That agreement is not universal. Paul Ramsey, for example, regards the methods and results of this period as a serious decline from the Oxford Conference of 1937. I shall refer to his criticisms later.[1] For the most part, however, it is held that a significant advance was made in these years.

Geneva to Uppsala

July 1966 saw the World Conference on Church and Society at Geneva which had been carefully prepared for from 1962. It followed logically upon the previous studies of rapid social change in Africa, Asia and Latin America by the Department on Church and Society of the World Council of Churches, but was on a much larger scale. Much of the preparatory work was embodied in four volumes of essays issued shortly before the conference.[2] In its last stages it had also been able to incorporate the work of two informal discussions on 'Theology and Social Ethics'[3] with Roman Catholics who had had some background part in the process which led to the Pastoral Constitution of the Second Vatican Council on 'The Church in the Modern World', generally known as *Gaudium et Spes*, which was passed at its final sessions in December 1965. In itself this was notable for its breadth, humanity and openness and for the fact that it was the first time a council of the church had ever addressed itself to such a theme.

There are at least five reasons for regarding the Geneva Conference as a breakthrough.

1. A conscious effort was made to ensure that it was as significant as the great Oxford Conference of 1937 on 'Church, Community and State', which was a landmark in the development of the ecumenical movement in its formative stages, and in the field of social ethics in the dark days of mass unemployment, Nazism and Fascism.

2. It was the first ecumenical conference, both in a global and in a church sense, in which the 'Third World' was so well represented that it could not be ignored. There were upwards of 400 present from over 70 countries, and among them black and brown skins were to be seen everywhere. There were not, unfortunately, enough yellow skins present, owing to the enforced lack of contact with China, but they were there from Japan and South-East Asia. It was impossible to carry on discussions of the 'Christian response to the technical and social revolutions of our time', which was the theme of the conference, in a Western context. Members from Western countries received many shocks and had rapidly to revise their perspectives. This was particularly true of those from the USA.

3. The Orthodox played a considerable part. The effect upon the World Council of Churches of the membership of leading Orthodox churches was evident. True, the Orthodox were at a disadvantage if they were not familiar with one of the Western European languages, for although Russian was one of the five official languages of the conference it was undeniably fifth in usefulness, and it was not easy for those whose language it was to intervene in the discussion with the freedom that most others enjoyed. But it was nevertheless impossible to carry on the discussion without a reminder of the weight of Orthodox Christian experience in the Communist world.

4. The Roman Catholic participant-observers, fresh from the work of the Second Vatican Council with its decree on Ecumenism and its Pastoral Constitution, played a full part in the work of the conference, and were sufficiently numerous to give a new ecumenical dimension to the discussions.

5. There was a very strong lay element present. Clergy and ministers did not in fact predominate. The considerable amount of expert theoretical knowledge and practical expertise available ensured that the conference could not take refuge in theological abstractions. Great and successful efforts had been made to persuade churches to select as nominees well-qualified lay people and not just ecclesiastical dignitaries. In fact, it proved

much harder to get laymen from the practical political field to come, or to stay the course, than it did from the world of economics and the social sciences, where the level of competence was very high. One can see why it was difficult when it is remembered that a British economic crisis broke out in the middle of it. This is clearly a permanent problem in ecumenical conferences.

No such ecumenical conference had ever been held before; and almost certainly no such radically-minded representative Christian conference had ever been held before. This is what the contemporary world does to those who face it as it is, and do not see it overwhelmingly through Western eyes. Furthermore the Christians present were brought face to face with things as they are now, not as they were some decades ago, or as we might prefer to think them to be.

If it had been an official church conference it would have been impossible to have had this composition; it would have been more Western and more clerical. It was possible for it to be as it was because the Central Committee of the World Council of Churches agreed to sponsor a conference which should be largely lay, expert, and representative of the 'Third World', and which would speak *to* the Council, not *for* it. This distinction has been attacked by Paul Ramsey as an invitation to irresponsible utterance, and I shall return to this, and to other criticisms, later. It is certainly not part of any claim that it was a breakthrough that it was beyond criticism.

Some of the notes it struck were indeed startling. But the fact that it did speak to the problems of our time as men experience them was indicated both by the broad resemblances between what it said and what the Second Vatican Council found it necessary to say in *Gaudium et Spes*,[4] and also by the fact that almost all the different departments of the World Council of Churches have begun to see their work in the perspective of the Geneva Conference. It is, for example, significant that the Faith and Order Department jointly sponsored a study conference with the Department on Church and Society to pursue further the theological issues lying behind the development of ecumenical social ethics. It saw that the unity of the church has to be seen in relation to the world in which the church is placed, a world in which the oneness of mankind is being forcibly brought home to us by rapid technological advances and the human consequences which follow from them. The consultation was held at Zagorsk, near Moscow, in 1968 and produced some important material.[5] In particular the consultation looked at the meaning and theological status of the term *revolution* which has come to be on everyone's lips.

Meanwhile one of the pre-Geneva consultations with Roman Catholics had said it was 'firmly convinced that there is no sufficient reason why further work on this theme (Christian Social Ethics) should be carried on in isolation, but rather that there ought to be consultation (or, as far as their ways of working will allow, collaboration) between the World Council of Churches and the Roman Catholic Church'. It was therefore appropriate that one upshot of the Geneva Conference and of the Second Vatican Council should be the setting up of an official joint Committee of the World Council of Churches and the Vatican Commission Justice and Peace; it covers the field of Society, Development and Peace and has in consequence come to be known as SODEPAX. It is so far the only official joint programme of the Roman Catholic Church and the World Council of Churches, and its potentialities are very great. Taking up the development issue it quickly sponsored an international expert consultation at Beirut in April 1968 'World Cooperation for Development', with the sub-title 'The Challenge to the Churches'. This and other work in the field of development and peace is now rapidly developing.[6]

Apart from this official follow-up of the Geneva Conference in the sphere of development, however, there was the question whether when it came to the Fourth Assembly of the World Council of Churches at Uppsala in July 1968 the official delegates of the churches would accept the general lines of the Geneva Conference when they were confronted with what it said *to* them, or whether they would find it too radical and disturbing. The delegates had before them all the material I have mentioned, and the Report of the Department on Church and Society. In the event they broadly endorsed it.[7] All the sectional reports of Uppsala are permeated by it, but especially that of Section III on 'World Economic and Social Development'.

The production of ecumenical documents and their authority

It is worth while considering the method of production and status of ecumenical texts such as those of Geneva and Uppsala. These consultations, conferences and assemblies are part of a

continuing movement with its own staff. The staff is chosen for
its sensitivity and alertness to what is going on in the church
and the world; and also to what is *not* going on in the church
but very probably ought to be. They are servants of their committees, and make a particular point of keeping in touch with
their chairman. The committees are made up of those chosen
by official church bodies for ecumenical assemblies, or are approved by them for a less formal conference if a name has been
put up to them asking for their approval. But a staff which is
on the job all the time is naturally in a strong position *vis-à-vis*
committee members who disappear to other preoccupations for
most of the year. By their travels they also have wider contacts
than most committee members. Out of the relationship between
staff and committee proposals emerge which are usually in the
first instance formulated by the staff. But they have to be agreed
to by official committees, not least in order to secure the finance
to implement them. Out of formal and informal discussions a
good deal of refinement goes on. In the end if a conference or
consultation is agreed to there will be a process of trial papers,
comments, revisions as a result of verbal and written comments,
perhaps consultative preparatory meetings, briefing of speakers
and group leaders, and finally the event itself.

The participants at the event may be chosen in various ways.
They may be direct delegates of official church bodies appointed
through legislative processes. This is, of course, especially the
case with an Assembly of the World Council of Churches. Or
they may be chosen in consultation with World Council staff
because of special qualifications or qualities required. Or they
may be directly nominated by the World Council. There are
other possible categories. The upshot is that the quality of
thought of any such conference is likely to be a good deal in
advance of the average level in any of the constituent churches.
Not merely is the membership carefully chosen and on the
whole well informed, but it is subject to the correction of
thought which comes from exposure to the reactions of those
from other confessions and areas of the world.

Once a conference is assembled it is likely to be split into
sections, and if large into sub-sections. The sub-sections may
be told to produce a draft report of approximately a certain
length in a certain time, perhaps three days. Problems of time
are acute. There are those of the adequacy of the interpretations,
even if competent simultaneous translation is available. It is not

always easy to secure this; and there is a good deal of scope for misunderstanding because of the variety of theological idioms and the wide range of subject matter, which can be very demanding on translators. Members of widely different confessional and global backgrounds and with widely different assumptions have to reach some kind of understanding and mutual confidence. Draft documents have to be drawn up and translated, revised, and again translated. Sub-section reports have to be incorporated in main section reports. These need revision. Mimeographing is required at every stage. Finally the material has to go to the whole conference. Pressures on drafters, translators and stenographers gets heavier and heavier as the conference nears its end. The whole conference has a relatively brief and broad discussion. There is probably dispute over a few points. Finally a document is given general approval and commended for study and action by the churches.[8]

It is a rough and ready process. One of the contributors to the symposium [*Technology and Social Justice*] has referred in a letter to 'confusions and compromises in documents drafted under intense pressure in all-too-brief, crowded and complex meetings, with representatives of different economic systems, cultures, ages, all articulate and insisting on voicing their conflicting points of view'. He adds that 'leisurely study and reflection on the direction and strength of, and gaps in, agreed statements is needed'. One of the sub-sections at the Geneva Conference spent almost all its time on hearing statements which its members who had come from different parts of the world were determined to give. There was little time for discussion. The rapporteur stayed up all night and, starting from these statements, produced a draft report of the sub-section which went through with acclaim and has survived practically unchanged in the final report. In another case a section had failed to provide in its discussions a theological framework for its report, and one member was asked to draft one. His free composition was accepted, with two improvements, and is in the Conference report, from which it is often quoted. Rough and ready, yes. But statements drawn up in this way do have broadly to commend themselves at every level of the conference. E. de Vries points out how often a consensus does emerge out of the initial divergences. Sometimes this is undoubtedly due to ambiguities in the wording of agreed statements, but this is only so in a small number of cases in the considerable body of texts of a conference like Geneva or the Assembly at Uppsala.

It is clear that much will depend on the selection of delegates, speakers and consultants. Here subjective factors are bound to have some influence in deciding which people and which points of view are significant. There is so much variety within the ecumenical movement that the biases of particular people and groups tend to cancel themselves out – but not entirely. No organization is infallible or immune from the sometimes ephemeral influences of the changing *Zeitgeist*, whether theological or in social thought. Those who are maintaining what may be an unfashionable position, or elaborating a new one, may feel that the whole enterprise is weighted against them. In any case where matters of expertise are concerned there is no *certain* way of distinguishing the pioneer or enthusiast from the crank.

For a long time the staff of the World Council of Churches was strongly influenced by the 'biblical theology' movement which came to the fore in the 1930s and of which Karl Barth was the major prophet. It has been taking some hard knocks in recent years and is now a shadow of what it was. One of its characteristics in its approach to ethical problems was its methodological arbitrariness. It certainly was not 'fundamentalist'. But the basis on which biblical texts were or were not used was never made clear. It had a fondness for moving from the Bible to some judgment about the modern world without any intervening steps in thought being made clear, or even without it being clear whether there were considered to be any intermediate steps. Many good things were said, and some not so good, but whether one agreed with them or not the basis on which they were arrived at remained obscure. One could not suppress the suspicion that the judgments were those of progressive twentieth-century Western European intellectuals and that suitable texts from the Bible were subsequently sought for as pegs on which to hang them. World Council documents on social ethics were full of this type of judgment. It seemed at times difficult for any other approach to get a look in. A similar experience has been the lot of those who wish to work within a 'natural law' ethic. It became a commonplace in ecumenical circles that the whole idea had been exploded, and it has been difficult to get it taken seriously. It has certainly been badly misused, and by those most attached to it, but it is hard to do without it in some form, as secular thinkers frequently discover, and it will have to be taken up again. Another example is the way in the last few years there has been general talk of a 'theology of hope' following upon the work of Moltmann and Pannenberg. There is no harm in this. New tendencies of thought often make their impact in an explosive fashion; but we must remember to scrutinize them with some care. The important thing is to keep open all channels of thought that are willing to associate with the ecumenical movement, and to seek to win over those which at present are not willing.

It is the temptation of 'Protestantism' to emphasize radical breaks with the past as it is of 'Catholicism' to emphasize continuity with it. Each has its dangers. The temptation of the World Council of Churches has been towards the former. It has not arisen where traditional confessional positions are in question; the Council is well schooled in seeing that all these get heard. It arises where theological tendencies and schools of thought are concerned which cut across confessional divisions; and there are more of them these days with the increasing pluralism within the confessions. There is no remedy except to be on guard against it, and to make a conscious effort to incorporate representatives of positions which those involved in planning World Council of Churches studies personally think to be mistaken.

When these qualifications are made, however, the ecumenical movement is astonishingly comprehensive. It seems to me, therefore, that documents coming out of its processes, rough and ready though they be, and receiving general approval, ought to possess a very high informal authority for the churches. One can of course say that the only test is who rightly discerns a word of truth, and whether a document comes from one man, a small group, a large one, an unofficial one, or an official one is irrelevant to the question of its truth. In the last resort this must be so, but short of that it is too simple a view. The fact that a large body of diverse and representative people have agreed to something makes it *prima facie* more significant than if it is the consensus of a small and perhaps self-selected group. That is why it is important that the Uppsala Assembly did not repudiate the work of the Geneva Conference. That conference, too, had its own level of authority as against, for example, a private and local gathering, because of the nature of its membership and the care in its preparation. Even individual papers which come from one person in one place and are then re-written after comment and criticism by others in different places and of different traditions, begin to carry considerable weight. But in the case of the Uppsala Assembly delegates formally appointed by the legislative processes of all the member churches in the World Council broadly endorsed the work of the Geneva Conference.

How else within the ecumenical movement can one secure an authoritative judgment on current questions of social ethics which have a world-wide reference? Where else in fact is it being secured? None of this work makes any claim to infallibility yet it surely shifts the onus on to those who disagree with it to justify their disagreement. If it has come through the fires of such a process and secured broad agreement it surely carries a certain presumption of cogency. The churches ought seriously to ask themselves whether they make enough use of it. There is evidence that the younger churches do, and that the 'established' churches of the 'West' do not. To them their domestic concerns loom larger, and ecumenical work tends to get what attention is left over after the former have had priority. Ecumenical work is usually in advance of where they have got to, and can conveniently be overlooked if it challenges cherished assumptions because they think themselves strong enough to do without it.

The situation slowly improves as the ecumenical movement grows. The churches are being led by the Spirit first to tolerate and then to approve a movement which has grown out of elements from within them and which acts as a goad and a spur to them. For centuries, ever since the breakdown of the medieval synthesis in fact, the tale has been of the churches trailing behind the changes in society or misunderstanding them. They have addressed themselves to problems of a past age without realizing it, or have failed to focus a problem correctly and therefore been ineffective because irrelevant. The history of church teaching on economic and social affairs is a good example of this. No tradition has come out well in its response to the Industrial Revolution. Now, for the first time for 500 years or more, the churches have been given a reasonably accurate and up-to-date picture of what is happening, what trends are at work, and the general direction in which Christian influence should be exercised. If they choose to hear they have the chance of acting relevantly. They cannot say that they have not had the chance to know.

Comparison with Roman Catholic documents

The only comparable documents are Roman Catholic ones. Only one in the field of social ethics, *Gaudium et Spes*, has come from a council; the rest are papal encyclicals. A brief comparison between them and documents of the World Council of Churches from the point of view of their authority may be useful. As we have seen, the latter class of documents commend themselves because of the global and inter-confessional discussion which has gone into their composition, and still more should the official delegates of the churches at an Assembly see their cogency and support them. Papal encyclicals appear to be very different in authority as they are in composition and tone. They are closely related to the understanding of the role of the *magisterium* in the Roman Catholic Church and the place of the papacy in it. They are prone to have a paternal and rotund style and to emphasize the constancy and authority of their teaching and the duty of the faithful to obey. Popes only quote their predecessors and classical Fathers of the church. The process by which judgments are reached is not usually known, nor what arguments led up to them. Sometimes the name of their main drafter or inspirer is known (in the case of *Casti Connubii* for instance) but by no means always. The background of *Humanae Vitae* is exceptional in the amount that is known of what led up to it, except for the final and crucial stages, the history of which is not known. But the way in which it was issued is significant for our present comparison. In the course of a long statement introducing the encyclical Monsignor Lambruschini said,

> The faithful know that the Pope, the successor of St Peter and Vicar of Christ, has a special assistance of the Holy Spirit which accompanies the mission of confirming in the faith and in the ways of the Lord all the members of the People of God, including the brothers in the episcopate. This assistance does not restrict itself to infallible definitions. . . . The pronouncement has come. It is not infallible but it does not leave the questions concerning birth regulation in a condition of vague problematics. Assent of theological faith is due only to the definitions properly so-called, but there is also loyal and full assent, interior and not only exterior, to an authentic pronouncement of the *magisterium*, in proportion to the level of authority from which it emanates – which in this case is the supreme authority of the Supreme Pontiff – and its object, which is most weighty since it is a matter of the tormented question of the regulation of births.
>
> In particular, it can and must be said that the authentic pronouncement of the *Humanae Vitae* encyclical prevents the forming of

a probable opinion, that is to say an opinion acting on the moral plane in contrast with the pronouncement itself, whatever the number and the hierarchical, scientific and theological authority of those who considered in the past few years that they could form it for themselves.

He went on to say that all those who had incautiously believed that they could teach anything different from what is in the encyclical must change their views and give full adhesion to its teachings.

As everyone knows, in spite of Monsignor Lambruschini's statement there has been a widespread objection to the encyclical from highly responsible theologians in the Roman Catholic Church, both as to its contents and the way in which it was produced. Episcopal conferences in several countries, notably Germany, Holland, Belgium, France and Canada, issued statements which came close to denying its teaching. So the question of the authority of this type of teaching in the church, that is to say of encyclicals, has come to the fore, and the situation is not as clear between them and official documents of the World Council of Churches as at first appears. There seems to have been a tendency in the Roman Catholic Church, in reaction to what it disliked in the nineteenth century, increasingly to stress the personal authority of the Pope. The First Vatican Council reflected this, and the tendency continued well into this century. For practical purposes all papal statements came to be given an aura of infallibility, and much was made of the steady, unchanging and certain teaching of the Roman Catholic Church on any matter she dealt with. The Conciliar movement of the Second Vatican Council and its aftermath has checked this and brought a different emphasis to the fore, without denying all that was in the earlier one. The reception of *Humanae Vitae* is one instance of this. Very detailed and agonized analyses have been made of the precise nature and degree of assent which it is required to give to an encyclical according to the varying degrees of difficulty or disagreement one may have with it. It has been realized that the authority of the papacy has been over-called and the constancy of its teaching and the extent to which it has been followed have been exaggerated. We have had detailed analyses of how papal teaching has changed on particular issues in the past, and of instances in which it has been ignored.

This discussion is not a weakness in the Roman Catholic

Church, it is a strength. The theory popular until recently was too rigid. In so far as it worked, which was never so far as was claimed for it, it could do so only in a static world. We are living in a pluralistic and rapidly changing one. There could be little likelihood of the papacy giving relevant advice or directions if the previous emphasis continued. That is why so many hope that as a result of the controversy occasioned by its appearance there will not be another *Humanae Vitae*. By contrast *Gaudium et Spes* was a much better document. And it was produced in a way much more like a document of the World Council of Churches. True, it was agreed to by a Council of all-male ecclesiastical persons, namely Bishops; but the delegates at a World Council Assembly are almost all ecclesiastical persons, either ordained or 'ecclesiastically-minded laymen', and overwhelmingly male. Further, the Second Vatican Council was able to call experts, again mostly in orders, as a World Council Assembly has its experts, though they are much less clerical and of a wider range, and youth is vociferously in the wings. Clearly the two are not the same, but their processes are not all that different in principle. It may be the case that the Roman Catholic Church is moving towards a way of producing church documents in the sphere of social ethics not unlike that of the World Council of Churches. It also has a possible theology of papal documents on the basis of which this could be done if it chose to use it. Perhaps the more it becomes associated with the one ecumenical movement the more this tendency will increase and papal authority come to be seen in a different way. Perhaps it will be seen more clearly that in the end the influence of papal documents depends upon their cogency being generally evident to the people of God, and the extent to which they draw upon the life of that people has a direct relation to that cogency being recognized. It certainly seems that the World Council of Churches is on the right lines in the process it adopts which finally leads to a document officially commended to the churches. There seems no other satisfactory way of setting about it.

Criticisms of ecumenical documents and procedures

This does not mean, however, that the execution of the process is beyond criticism. Some criticisms have already been noted, and there are others which deserve to be weighed. Some are mentioned elsewhere in the symposium. Savramis is by no means wholly critical, but he charges the World Council of Churches with being satisfied with empty formulas, compromises and clichés; and in particular with a desire to be 'with it' and conform to the latest 'pop theology' in vogue. Schmémann is entirely negative and his criticisms are similar. He charges the Council with an *a posteriori* theological method, which begins with a this-worldly outlook of a utopian and semi-Marxist character and then looks for odd biblical texts to justify it, theological criteria having had no controlling influence. In particular the talk of all things becoming new ignores God's newness. A correspondent, from a different confessional background, accuses the World Council's work of being 'based on a situation ethic combined with a mild and unsophisticated idea of human dignity and happiness'. These criticisms cannot be brushed aside. Every reader can judge for himself from the text of Uppsala, Section III, and these essays related to it how far they are justified. At any rate they point to obvious dangers against which it is necessary to be on the alert. Yet it would be odd if all the weighty delegates from so many different churches should have fallen so completely into these errors attributed to them. Several contributers to the symposium suggest that their work can be seen in a much more favourable theological light. On this division of opinion two comments may be made. The first is that it is perfectly possible to start from the other end, from formally correct theological positions, from full credal orthodoxy, and still arrive at conclusions regarding this world which are irrelevant or even corrupt, because of failure adequately to grapple with empirical reality and, maybe, because of material vested interests in the *status quo* which lead to a quite unjustified support being given to it. Indeed this is precisely what has often happened in Christian history. To take one example, no one would accuse the church in Russia of heretical tendencies, and yet it explicitly or tacitly supported remediable evils for so long and to such an extent that it took the violence of the Bolshevik revolution with its equally one-sided stress and its many errors to induce the Russian people to tackle them.

The aim, of course, is not to begin either with formal theology or with the current empirical situation, but with both at once: it is to let one interact with the other, thereby allowing theology to use its categories to analyse the data of this world and our responsibilities in it; and the data of this world to call in question theological irrelevancies and abstractions. Ideally everyone would be equally competent to begin at either end. In fact some have one particular expertise, some another and some can move competently in more than one. There are many varying proportions of competence. That is why a co-operative effort is needed.

The second thing to be said is that there is often a great gulf between the way a trained theologian and an informed layman expresses himself when considering social and economic life in the light of the Christian faith. The layman often, indeed usually if he is sufficiently prominent in his church to be a delegate on ecumenical occasions, thinks in Christian categories but does not express them in a technical theological vocabulary. The theologian is at home in this but may not think about this world with any great precision or assurance. In conferences and consultations the two are intended to blend their contributions. But when this problem is added to those of differences of global and confessional background, and of language, it is possible to achieve this only to a partial extent in the time available. Many agreed documents do not necessarily express precisely the fullness of the theological insights which lie behind them, nor do they always achieve niceties of technical theological expression. It is important not to read them in too external a fashion. This is not, needless to say, an excuse for theological frivolity or an easy conformism to the *Zeitgeist*, against which alertness is always necessary.

The most weighty criticism, however, of the method of ecumenical social ethics has come from Paul Ramsey in his appraisal of the Geneva Conference, *Who Speaks for the Church?*[9] He is by no means entirely critical and, indeed, holds that much of its work is 'astonishingly good', but he concentrates on the points on which he is critical. These are concerned with what he was personally involved in himself, the general meetings and his section and sub-section. Whether he would have been as critical of the other sections and sub-sections one cannot tell. It seems by implication that he is reasonably satisfied with Section I, which corresponds to Uppsala, Section III. Some of his criticisms cover the method of procedure in producing documents, which we have already mentioned. Another relates to the unwisdom of a study conference wanting to pass so many resolutions, many of them on detailed and involved issues of policy. Here he has a strong case.[10] Again he alleges that the conference was theologically slanted in terms of 'truncated Barthianism', or what in the same paragraph he calls a 'contextual revolutionary-christocentric eschatologism', as distinct from a theology that follows the sequence of the creed – creation, law and ordinances, then gospel – which has been well represented in ecumenical ethics hitherto.[11] He has a point here, whether or not he has precisely succeeded in putting his finger on what seemed the most vocal theological stance. Certainly a separate group on Christian Social Ethics (which was given absurdly little time in which to work, in the spare intervals of supposedly free afternoons) saw a quick Lutheran reaction on similar lines, which there was no time adequately to discuss, and which was simply printed as a separate statement.[12]

Ramsey's main criticism, however, is against a whole type of pronouncement on policy questions found in the work of the conference. Instead of *basic* decisions and action-oriented *principles* of ethical and political analysis, the conference continually went on to make particular pronouncements on policy questions based on assertions on 'what God is doing in the world', which could be highly disputable, and without making clear the cost implications of the policies advocated. The result was, Ramsey maintains, that ill-thought-out solutions to particular problems which ought to be settled by prudence and worldly wisdom were put forward on an allegedly Christian basis. Christians who disagreed were implicitly put in the wrong and held to have a faulty conscience.

Ramsey entirely agrees that purely general statements are not enough. They give a spurious air of making a contribution to a problem when in fact they have not enough content for anyone to have anything to disagree with. They are like being 'against sin'.[13] On the other hand to my mind the objection to particular policy conclusions being invested with a Christian aura is that they are bound to depend upon an interpretation of what are the facts, the weightage to be given to different facts, and the trends, and the likely consequences of possible lines of action in a particular empirical situation. About all of these there can in the nature of the case be no certainty, and therefore differences of opinion are likely. This does not mean that the church can *never* make an explicit policy recommendation; it is to say that it is not the typical thing for it to do. Ramsey agrees that in an exceptional situation, such as 'before the gates of Auschwitz', the church may have to take a stand on a precise point, though he adds that if the churches are more effective all the time things may not get to such a desperate pass.[14] But in general churches should aim to speak at a middle level halfway between general statements and political policies. This is the level at which the Oxford Conference of 1937 operated, the level which it called that of 'middle axioms', though the term – drawn by analogy from logic – may not be a particularly good one. Two quotations will give the flavour of Ramsey's argument:

> Christians, meeting as such, should not allow themselves to advocate particular problems in the public forum without also specifying how we are to get from where we are.[15]
>   It is high time for it to be acknowledged on all sides that not every decision is a moral decision, and not every moral decision a Christian decision. The bearing of God's will and governance in relation to every aspect of life cannot possibly be construed in such a fashion that supposes that there is a Christian shape or style to every decision. Concerning a great many choices it has to be said that only a deliberately or inflexibly imprudent decision would be wrong, or an uncharitable exercise of prudence.[16]

Ramsey finds a good instance of what he advocates in a statement of the Archbishop of Canterbury at the time of the Rhodesian rebellion under Ian Smith against Britain. There was division in British opinion. The churches in exercising their public responsibility were right to find a word to say. Some people were pressing for military force to be used against Rhodesia to compel multi-racial guarantees before recognizing its independence. Speaking on behalf of the British Council of Churches the Archbishop said,

> It is not for us as Christian Churches to give our Government military advice as to what is practicable or possible. . . . If [the Prime Minister] and his Government think it necessary to use force for the perpetuation of our existing obligations in Rhodesia, then a great body of Christian opinion in this country will support him in so doing.

That is to say, Christian support was given to certain ends; the question of means was not left out, but whether a particular one should be used was left to those in authority to determine.

There are still elements of disputable specificity in the Archbishop's statement, and Ramsey is prepared to admit that there is only a relative distinction between a statement in the realm of middle axioms or middle principles and a specific one. Nevertheless, the distinction is important. His aim is clear. He wants

to avoid merely giving religious sanction to feelings and prejudice, and to achieve objectivity, prudence and rationality in
judgment. To this end he wants to stay as far as possible within
the middle principle of ethical decision and analysis arrived at
by reflection upon the basic features of Christian faith and
doctrine. Yet the admission that if these are to bear on a particular situation and not be purely theoretical *some* element of
empirical analysis must enter is crucial. There seems no reason
in principle why these middle axioms (as referred to by J. H.
Oldham at the Oxford Conference and taken up in subsequent
years)[17] should not go further than Ramsey's illustration does,
provided general agreement to the empirical analysis can be secured. If church bodies get together groups of people on particular problems with the relevant background and experience
and if a consensus develops as to the relevant facts and their
weightage, and as to the likely consequences of possible courses
of action, so that on the basis of Christian judgment they suggest the directions in which Christian efforts should be mobil-
ized, there is no need to limit or prescribe the amount of detail
in the recommendations they may come to, even though it is
unlikely that it will get as far as detailed specific policies. If
there is no agreement recommendations cannot be formulated.
In any event they will need periodic checking as time goes by
and the situation changes. This is what the ecumenical movement to a considerable extent has been doing, but it has not
made this sufficiently clear since Amsterdam. In so far as it fails
it may be due to too great a division of opinion (which cannot
be helped); or that a not sufficiently representative cross-section
of relevant opinion has been consulted, so that any agreement
is in fact partial; or because of a sheer failure in procedure and
technique in carrying out conferences and consultations. In particular it has not sufficiently made clear the implications and
limitations of the 'what God is doing in the world' approach.

If conclusions are properly arrived at they do not unchurch
those who disagree. What they do is to put the onus on them
to produce cogent reasons for disagreeing with the consensus,
rather than the onus being the other way round. They are
extremely useful for at least six reasons.

1. As a help to the individual Christian in his own decisions.
2. As a link between those of different confessions.
3. As a potential link between Christians and those of other
faiths and none.

4. As a dissolver of the division between the parson and the layman, for the experience of both is needed to formulate them.

5. As a stimulus to creating a bad conscience when society, and perhaps the church as a whole, is complacent.

6. In helping the church to achieve some purchase over events and not lag behind them.

In making any such statements church studies need to think very clearly who is being asked to do what, at what cost, and why. If they do so, and succeed in producing relevant and responsible statements, they can make a valuable contribution to the political community by putting decision in a wider context, taking care to bring out facts which public opinion or governments or both may wish to avoid, and calling for the kind of justice which is the expression of love at the corporate level.[18]

Ramsey is formally correct in his exposition of middle axioms but has a too restricted view of their possible scope. His approach is clearly very close to a renewed Lutheran 'two realms' doctrine; indeed he may be said to have shown very usefully how it can be renewed. But just as it has generally been interpreted too negatively, so Ramsey is too negative in tone and temper. Maybe the fact that he did not like a good many of the particular conclusions of Geneva is the reason for this. If the onus is on those who dissent from a consensus to show why, he certainly goes into considerable detail to make the grounds of his disagreement plain on several issues. Not everything done at Geneva was well done. Subsequent reflection will show what has to be discarded.

Ramsey finds the root cause of which he considers ill-founded specific judgments in the tendency to jump to particular conclusions on the basis of what God is doing in the world. It was never made clear at Geneva what were the canons of judgment by which out of all the things happening in the world some were to be given the status of God's doing, and how such statements were to be delivered from a capricious situationism. Some seemed to think that he was solely making revolutions. Often the appeal was to 'prophetic religion', to the Old Testament prophets who for example would move directly from 'thus says the Lord' to a conclusion about foreign policy, perhaps a projected alliance. But in this and other respects it is a mistake to move too quickly from the Old Testament to the New, or we shall be like the English Reformers who saw in Henry VIII the

equivalent of the godly prince David, and some of whose successors a century later justified the execution of Charles I by
reference to the source in the book of Samuel which represents
the desire of Israel for a king as disloyalty to Yahweh. Prophetic
religion in the Old Testament was related to a state which was
also a church, a people of God, a covenant community. In the
New Testament that situation is split wide open. The people of
God has now become a universal community; church and state
are no longer one community, whether the church is established
or not. St Augustine was quite clear that the fact that Christianity had become the adopted religion of the Roman state did
not mean that there were no longer two cities but one. The city
of God and the earthly city remained distinct. The injunction to
discern the signs of the times remains an on-going task. Basic
moral requirements of justice and the righteousness which is
on the side of the needy and oppressed remain the same (would
that the church had remembered this more effectively!). But the
exercise of prophetic faith cannot be in precisely the Old Testament way. Basic Christian faith and contemporary insight are
not on the same level. One cannot pass from what God is doing
to a particular decision in the same breath. A basic Christian
understanding of life has to be brought alongside an empirical
situation. From the former broad criteria are available: the application involves the element of empirical analysis and the
inevitable hazards we have been discussing.

Ramsey has a final criticism which is not well founded. He is
altogether opposed to the method of churches sponsoring conferences whose members will not speak *for* them but *to* them,
who are officially convened to speak unofficially. Geneva was
an outstanding example of this. He says, 'One can scarcely
imagine a situation that to a greater extent invites irresponsible
utterance.'[19] In this he is surely mistaken. Official church bodies, largely made up of dignitaries of various kinds and
ecclesiastically-minded laymen (all of them properly employed
when carrying out their normal church duties), are not the best
to investigate and reflect initially on the manifold empirical
situation. Once other conferences and consultations have done
their work the official bodies can weigh it and speak *for* the
churches. That was precisely the relation of Geneva to Uppsala.
It is true that less official bodies may be tempted to irresponsi-
bility; the remedy is to guard against it, not to abolish them.

What other method is there? Ramsey proposes several sessions of the same council over a period of years. Only by this means, he thinks, will the theologians and the secular expert come to understand one another. He clearly has in mind the four sessions of seven weeks of the Fathers of the Second Vatican Council 1962–65, together with their attendant *periti*. But the suggestion is utterly impracticable. The Vatican Council was very costly. And it was composed almost entirely of bishops. How could a conference with the number and quality of the laymen at Geneva meet for several weeks for several years? Problems of time as well as money are insuperable. As it was it was a hard task to assemble and keep them together for one fortnight.

The ecumenical movement is bound to work under severe limitations of time and money. Its processes are bound to be rough and ready and open to criticism. There is no reason for complacency. Criticisms must be attended to, weighed, and what is valid in them, guarded against within the limits of practicability. When all is said, however, Geneva was a landmark which is likely to stand out in the church history of this century. Together with what followed in the two-year period 1966–68 at Zagorsk, Beirut and Uppsala, it marked an important advance in ecumenical social ethics. Time is rapidly sifting what was not well founded. We can thank God for all that remains.

3

Middle Axioms in Christian Social Ethics

An underlying issue in the increasing concern for Christian social ethics is how far and with what justification the Christian faith can provide guidance about detailed and specific decisions as distinct from giving a fundamental insight into human life and destiny. We get a pretty clear picture from the New Testament of the qualities of a Christian life, for instance St Paul's list of the fruit of the Spirit in Galatians 5, but how do they bear on specific ethical problems, and in particular on the collective affairs of men? Further, in what way can guidance or instruction be given in these matters by church bodies of an official or semi-official character?

After the Geneva Conference of the World Council of Churches on 'Church and Society' in 1966, Paul Ramsey of Princeton University wrote a criticism of it, *Who Speaks for the Church?*[1] in which he raised very sharply the two-fold question 'Who Speaks?' and 'How do they speak?'. At a much less sophisticated level, however, there remains a good deal of unease, sometimes expressed in such a phrase as 'politics and religion don't mix', or more specifically 'I don't like to hear politics from the pulpit'. Yet Christians can see that such a simple dichotomy will not do, for it plays straight into the hands of totalitarian governments who will tolerate a church so long as it confines itself to an individualistic and other-worldly piety leaving the powers that be to deal with the world. Nevertheless a sense of unease remains that the basic truths of the Christian faith and detailed policies are not on the same level, and that the distinction between them should be kept clear.

On the other hand there is also a widespread feeling that the church ought to have something to say on current issues in debate, whether it be the sale of arms to South Africa or the character of TV programmes. The problem is how whatever organ of the church which does say something can avoid harmless generalities on the one side, or the endorsing of very particular and often highly disputable policies on the other. They are disputable because they involve a whole series of judgments about the facts of an issue, and the possible consequences of different lines of action, about which there are inescapable uncertainties (if only because we cannot foresee with certainty), and therefore more than one possible opinion.

Both characteristics are frequently found in church statements. The more common is a desire to speak significantly but to take refuge in statements of such generality as to be vacuous. At one time I made a collection of examples. Here are two. One of them urges men 'to promote increasing co-operation between individuals and groups in all phases of economic life'. The other says, 'the real needs and just demands of nations should be benevolently examined'. It is hardly possible to disagree with them because they do no more than commend good will. They are against sin. Sometimes they can appear to be specific and yet remain vacuous; an example is a resolution on Vietnam of the 1966 Geneva Conference which said that hostilities and military action should be stopped and the conditions created for a peaceful settlement. The same conference was in danger of passing a detailed resolution on the Rhodesian rebellion against Britain which was based on misinformation. Having been baulked on this, and yet being determined to say something, it evaded a problem by passing an unrealistic motion that the whole matter be handed over to the United Nations. Yet another way is to pass a resolution which is ambiguous and which protagonists of opposing views then interpret in different ways.

A method of avoiding these courses was adumbrated in the preliminary volume issued to all those attending the Oxford Conference on 'Church Community and State' in 1937, which is rightly considered a landmark in the recovery of an adequate method in Christian social ethics. The book, *The Church and its Function in Society*, was by W. A. Visser 't Hooft and J. H. Oldham.[2] Among other things it discusses the need to arrive at some middle ground between general statements and detailed policies. On page 210 it refers to what it calls 'middle axioms'. It describes them as 'an attempt to define the directions in which, in a particular state of society, Christian faith must express itself. They are not binding for all time, but are provisional definitions of the type of behaviour of Christians in a given period and given circumstances.' The idea was taken up by William Temple in his Introduction to the Malvern Conference volume 1941, and by the war-time Church of Scotland Report on 'The Interpretation of God's Will in our Time'. It is discussed by John Bennett in *Christian Ethics and Social Policy* 1946 (the title of the British edition was *Christian Social Action*[3]). And there is an interesting footnote by Reinhold Niebuhr in an essay in the Amsterdam volume, *The Church and the Disorder of Society* issued after the first General Assembly of the World Council of Churches in 1948, where he says, 'The Oxford Conference sought to find a middle ground between a Christian view which offered no general directives to the Christian with regard to social and political institutions, and the view which tried to identify the mind of Christ too simply with specific economic social and political programmes. For the ecumenical movement, in the opinion of many, this middle ground is still the proper basis of approach.'[4]

John Bennett gives several illustrations of middle axioms. Two in the economic field are (*i*) the government has the responsibility of maintaining full employment; (*ii*) private centres of economic power should not be stronger than the government. The point now is not whether these are agreed, relevant or meaningful, but merely that they are illustrations of suggested Christian policies which are neither simply general, nor detailed, but halfway between; in short, in the middle.

I am not aware of any discussions of them since 1948, but that does not mean that they have faded out. Quite a lot of work done by the Board for Social Responsibility of the Church Assembly (now the General Synod), the Methodist Christian Citizenship Department, the British Council of Churches and the World Council of Churches has in fact been in this middle region. It does not matter whether the name is used or not. It is, however, worthwhile to look explicitly at the idea of middle axioms, their nature and authority, in the cause of greater coherence in Christian social ethics, and not least because there are other and less satisfactory ways of bridging the gap between the fundamentals of the faith and the immediate situation. We will look briefly at these at the end.

Middle axioms are arrived at by bringing alongside one another the total Christian understanding of life and an analysis of an empirical situation. The Christian understanding of life involves all the elements of an articulated theology which have arisen in the church out of reflection on the witness to Christ in the Bible. It includes a picture of the proper way of life, personal and social, which follows from the Christian faith. On this all Christians will broadly agree, though doubtless there will be different theological emphases. The Christian way of life is so far-reaching that it transcends any particular embodiment either in personal life or social structures. When we look at an empirical situation our job is to establish the facts and the underlying trends, and to ask where the Christian understanding of life is particularly being disregarded. A middle axiom is formed to indicate the general direction in which action should be taken to improve the situation. Here we enter upon a debatable area. Our factual enquiry is open to all the hazards of trying to ascertain facts. (The Christian has no privileged position over any other citizen in this task; he has to do his homework like anyone else.) On the other hand the Christian brings a distinctive understanding of life which may lead him to see facts differently and weigh them differently from others, because significant facts are always seen in a wider context. Sometimes he may not see them differently. Christians and humanists, for instance, often share an outlook in common to a considerable extent. But not always. Some of the recent disagreements on abortion law clearly arise out of a different understanding of facts between some Christians and some humanists. With middle axioms we are at a halfway stage between what is clear Christian judgment and what is an opinion subject to empirical hazards and checks. To get to a detailed policy recommendation would be to go much further towards the latter.

If middle axioms can be arrived at, how authoritative are they? They cannot be 'of faith' because they involve an element of empirical judgment on a specific situation. On the other hand they can only be arrived at if they represent a good cross-section of relevant opinion. Thus they do carry high informal authority. Within one country if a representative group arrives at a consensus it carries more weight than if only one confessional tradition does. If a consensus is reached within the World Council of Churches, crossing national and confessional boundaries on a world scale, that is more impressive. Should the Roman

Catholic Church and the WCC achieve a consensus that is the most weighty of all. All the more significant, therefore, for Christians is the similarity between so much of the Geneva Conference of 1966 and the Pastoral Constitutions of the Second Vatican Council, *Gaudium et Spes*, and the joint work on 'Society, Development and Peace' which has sprung from it. Perhaps we can say that middle axioms shift the burden of proof. The onus is on those who disagree to make out a good case for their disagreement rather than the other way round.

How detailed can they be? It is impossible to say precisely, except that they do not go as far as policy formulation. This is not to say that church bodies should never be specific and detailed, but the occasions will be rare; what Paul Ramsey calls 'before the gates of Auschwitz'. For the most part church bodies as such should hesitate to rush in with a detailed policy on each controversy as it occurs. It is better to try to disentangle the issues, indicate the areas of judgment and the range of possible actions (perhaps excluding one or more as impermissible), and looking out for inconvenient aspects of the problem which the government or the community or both is inclined to gloss over. In this way the church can then help Christians in the first instance, and often the community at large, to make informed judgments. But we are concerned here with the degree of particularity of middle axioms. All one can say is that the more detailed they are, the more dated they are likely to be by the time they have got over to the Christian public, let alone the general public. For they need to be under constant revision as circumstances change. Moreover the means used to correct an unfavourable judgment on the *status quo* will sooner or later lead to a new situation and consequences which in turn will need correction by a new middle axiom.

Of course no one – not even the theologian – can stop at the level of middle axioms. As citizens we have to support detailed policies in the direction they indicate. Here many differences between Christians will arise. Two equally sincere Christians in agreement about a middle axiom may disagree as to how it is best implemented by particular policies, perhaps because of different estimates of the probable consequences of them. There is an irreducible uncertainty in life which is reflected in Christian ethics. It is chiefly for this reason that political parties and trade unions with the name 'Christian' in their title are best avoided. We can be glad that we do not have them in this country.

Some may think all this rather disappointing and something of a damp squib. But middle axioms do have many advantages. I can think of eight.

1. They are a help to the individual Christian in making his own decisions, as citizen and perhaps in his job.

2. They are a link between different confessions. For the most part there does not seem much point in the different churches 'going it alone' in this enterprise.

3. They are a link between Christians and non-Christians in facing a common problem. The expertise of non-Christians can often and usefully be brought into the discussions out of which they arise.

4. They give the Christian community something to say relevant to the concerns of the general public.

5. They are useful in breaking down the clerical-lay division in the church. They cannot be arrived at by clergy or by theologians alone. Relevant lay experience is absolutely essential.

6. They can help to create a bad conscience where people are complacent, whether in the church or the community at large. It is no accident that they arise out of a negative judgment on the *status quo*. For instance in so far as equality is a concept having relevance (among others like justice, freedom, order) to a Christian understanding of a humane society – and it certainly has some place though it is extraordinarily difficult to define exactly what we mean by it – we understand it and its implications better by seeing where it is being markedly infringed than by approaching it directly.

7. They help the church to take some purchase over events, and not lag far behind with an irrelevant message. We cannot be too grateful for the work of the ecumenical movement in social ethics which has enabled the churches to be up to date, in the sense of knowing what is happening, for the first time since the Industrial Revolution accelerated the speed of social change.

8. They help the church to avoid either the pietism which takes no interest in this world, or the perfectionism which can only deal in absolutes and therefore never has a relevant word to those who have to do the best possible in tangled situations, and in structures of life in which God has placed us alongside others of all faiths with whom we have to work, and which cannot pre-suppose a shared Christian faith as a basis for their working.

In view of all this one would hope to see continuous efforts made by the churches to get together different groups of people with different confessional, occupational and, where appropriate, national backgrounds, to keep abreast of the different areas of life. As we have seen, this is being done to some extent, but there is a lot of scope for more. In the professions, for instance, only teaching is well catered for; medicine and social work much less so, industry and commerce only sporadically. Further the churches are not good at feeding the work they have sponsored into their own life. The attention paid by the church in this country to the very important Geneva Conference of 1966 has been minimal. And few Anglicans know of the excellent work done in recent years by groups convened by their own Board for Social Responsibility. There is abundant material here for sermons and church groups of all kinds.

In conclusion the significance of middle axioms can be seen by a brief reference to three other ways of arriving at church pronouncements, none of them satisfactory. One is to make a detailed pronouncement on the basis of an *a priori* deduction from an alleged maxim of Natural Law. This has been characteristic of much Roman Catholic and some Anglican social teaching. The papal encyclical *Humanae Vitae* is a recent instance. Here the Pope arrived at a detailed conclusion that various forms of contraception are 'unnatural' on an *a priori* basis. (This is the root of the encyclical though, because the conclusion lacks the self-evidence that in theory it ought to have, he brings in church authority to back up his verdict of 'unnatural' and he further adds logically irrelevant and in fact weak empirical arguments.) The question of Natural Law is a vast and complex one. All we say here is that this way of using what is a necessary concept is growingly discredited, not least in Roman Catholic moral theology itself. One can dare to be an optimist and hope that there will be no successors to *Humanae Vitae*.

Another position is that of an extreme Lutheran interpretation of the doctrine of the two kingdoms. On this view the kingdom of God's left hand (the orders of society) is so sharply separated from the kingdom of his right hand (the church) that it can get no guidance from the Christian faith. This extreme autonomy is viewed with growing disfavour in Lutheran circles. Hitler was a great shock to it. Lutherans are now engaged in expressing the two kingdoms doctrine in a way which allows for a Christian light to be thrown on the structures of society, as

Roman Catholics are beginning to stress a view of Natural Law which allows for empirical data.

A third position, which springs more from a Calvinist background, is to want to go direct from the Bible to a specific conclusion on a contemporary issue. There has been a good deal of this in WCC documents, especially in the now faded era of 'biblical theology'. Karl Barth was an unfortunate influence in this respect. Because Jesus Christ is the light of the world there must be no secret diplomacy. Because Jesus Christ has risen from the dead Hitler must be resisted. Such a procedure never escapes from the arbitrary; and there is always the possibility of other Christians making the same incomprehensible leap from a particular text to a different conclusion. The latest example of this approach are the Christians who claim to be able to move directly from a Christian perspective to say what God is doing in the world. Apparently he is always creating revolutions and never conserving. To thank him for 'creation, preservation and all the blessings of this life' is outmoded. This approach springs from a desire to have too unambiguous a Christian word for empirical situations. It is fond of quoting the Old Testament prophets and forgets that in the Christian dispensation there are *two* kingdoms, whereas in the old dispensation there was only one. Israel was both state and church.

By comparison the method of middle axioms is sounder. It is critical of the *status quo*, but it keeps contingent political and social judgments in their proper and necessary but secondary place. It requires Christian social action and will not sanction a private pietism, but it differentiates between God's cause and our causes. It takes the religious overtones out of politics whilst insisting that it is a necessary area of Christian obedience. The fact that we have a long way to go before the Christian community has grasped this and followed it is a reason for taking the method of the middle axiom approach seriously.

4

On the Theological Fringe

Sometimes it is useful for a speaker to be given a title; it acts as a challenge and a stimulus to his thought. This is certainly the case when a newly appointed Professor of Social and Pastoral Theology is invited to explain what he is up to, under the title 'On the Theological Fringe'.[1] Are those who suggested it, he wonders, merely referring to the facts of his position *vis-à-vis* the weight of theological studies in Britain? If so, they are right. Or are they perhaps inferring that this is where he is appropriately to be put? In that case their opinion must be disputed. Or could it be that they think the fringe is the best place to be? That would show a considerable degree of theological discernment which would greatly encourage him.

'Fringe' suggests other words of similar import. My dictionary suggests 'border' or 'borderline'. Other possibilities are 'boundary', 'frontier' and 'margin'. Perhaps the last would only occur to an economist. In the pure theory of the market it is the marginal unit, the marginal increment which is the one of decisive significance. 'Frontier' reminds us of the work of the Christian Frontier Council, and of the growth of specialist chaplaincies as, for instance, in industry; it brings to mind the talk of 'dialogue' and of the 'Christian presence' which we have heard frequently in the past two decades. 'Boundary' is a word peculiarly associated with Paul Tillich. His earliest work to be translated into English in 1935, *The Interpretation of History*, contained an autobiographical section called 'On the Boundary'. The translation was a bad one, and this section was newly translated and issued by itself in the USA in 1966 and in this country a year later.[2] In it Tillich distinguishes thirteen boundary positions which made up his life. Three of them, to quote examples, are (*i*) between theory and practice (*i.e.*, he cannot accept either the idealist or the Marxist position on the relation between the two); (*ii*) between church and society; (*iii*) between religion and culture. 'The boundary', he says, 'is the best place for acquiring knowledge.' Thielicke in his *Theological Ethics* echoes Tillich but uses the term 'borderline' instead of 'boundary'; 'the borderline is the truly propitious place for acquiring ethical knowledge'.[3] In this he echoes Brunner who two decades earlier remarked that it is on the borderline between economics and politics on the one hand and theology on the other, that the great decisions are made; he added 'if the theology fails here it fails all along the line'.

Tillich, however, is the foremost modern theologian in ability to make the most of the boundary situation. No other known to me has had such an extensive personal acquaintance with so wide a range of human knowledge and creativity. Apart from philosophy and theology, which were of course his main concern, he was at home in psychology and sociology, and in poetry, novels, plays, painting, sculpture and to a lesser extent, music. He could think theologically about them, not merely from outside, but illuminate them so to speak from within, and so produce what for want of a better term we may call a theology of culture. This is necessary. We all know that any synthesis of the mediaeval type, with theology as 'the queen of the sciences', is no longer possible. We have learned that the autonomy of each area of study and of the arts must be respected. The intellectual core of each discipline must be respected; and the artist must respect his materials. Yet to be satisfied with a complete fragmentation of life is a counsel of despair. It is also hardly possible. Human beings in practice have some intellectual map, and see what on the surface appear to be purely neutral facts within some frame of reference. Sometimes this is avowed (as in religions or substitute religions like Marxism); sometimes it is unavowed (as in some types of humanist frames of reference which think of themselves as 'neutral' or 'scientific' as opposed to a faith). It is the task of the Christian to show that his frame of reference makes the best sense of life as we know it in living it. This means relating it critically and constructively to other frames of reference and, more important, thinking theologically about the different spheres of human life in a way which respects their autonomy and allows them to react reciprocally with theology. This is what Tillich did with his 'method of co-relation' and in my view it was his most significant achievement.

Another way of making the same point is to call for a renewed and reformed natural theology. One thinks of Professor Root's stimulating opening essay in the symposium *Soundings*[4] which laments the disengagement of Christian theology from the creative imagination of our time, and ends abruptly just where it has become exciting.

Social and pastoral theology, itself a provisional title, seems clearly to fall within the broader framework of a theology of culture, since it is specially concerned with the social context of the religious life of the country locally, nationally and internationally; this includes the structures of industry, economic life, politics and citizenship. This is a field in which Reinhold Niebuhr has perhaps made the chief theological contribution in this century, and in view of his recent death it is good to remind ourselves of this. But this is not the whole field of a theology of culture, and one would hope that more systematic theologians would see it as of prime importance.

How does social and pastoral theology fit into the general pattern of theological studies? Perhaps a little theological mapwork may be useful, even though one can't be too tidy with it; the complexities of the intellectual scene resist precise classification. We can regard theology in a general way as systematic thought about a religious faith. (In a fuller discussion both the terms 'religion' and 'faith' would require investigation.) In this country that faith is predominantly the Christian faith. We will refer to others later. The basic study of it is an honours or pass degree course, or some substitute, whilst particular applications of it in depth are suitable for post-graduate diplomas, like the diplomas in pastoral theology which have lately begun to be established. The basic discipline has two sides to it: acquiring the intellectual tools and learning to use them. There are further distinctions which could be made about the relation of the two, but for our present purposes the broad distinction will do.

In England far more attention has been paid to acquiring the tools than to using them. Theology as a study has been rooted in the critical and historical study of the Bible. This is because of the Anglican and Protestant tradition of the country with its particular emphases on holy scripture. Roman Catholics have been entirely outside the university study of theology until very recently. Had they been in it the Bible would not have been neglected, but the study of it would have been put in a different framework. The fact that they are now beginning to join in university studies is to be unreservedly welcomed. The concentration on biblical studies has been accentuated by the content of agreed syllabuses of religious education in schools, so that the provision of those suitably qualified to teach them has often been referred to simply as the production of 'scripture specialists'. To these studies a little history of doctrine and church history has traditionally been added, especially up to 451, covering the crucial early years of the Christian church in the world out of which it came. This was all the more natural because theological studies were closely related to classical studies, and understandably so in view of the place of Greek in early Christian sources; but it was strengthened by the fact that classical studies were the basic university education of the English 'gentlemen', and for a long time it was thought no other specific training was needed for ordination in the Church of England. When this attitude began to break down it was natural to presuppose that classicial studies had preceded the new theological studies. But all this adds up to a prolegomenon to theology rather than theological study itself. Tools are acquired but not the training in using them.

At least two factors have made skill in using the tools more important. One is growth in the intellectual challenges to the Christian position. Whether they are more or less great than in the last three centuries may be arguable, but their growth in influence seems undisputed. For example, it is no longer adequate to send highly qualified teachers as religious education specialists into the upper forms of secondary schools if their training has been overwhelmingly biblical, because the pupils are not prepared in advance to accept the privileged status of the Bible. The second new factor is the growth of a plural society instead of the broadly homogeneous one of the 'Christendom' situation. Not only are significant numbers of adherents of other religions living among us, but we also know much more about them globally. Further, the development of the social sciences has made us much more aware of social processes in human life.

For these reasons more and more studies are gradually being added to the theological curriculum. Nothing dramatic has happened, certainly nothing like what has happened in the USA. But the comparative study of religions is all the time gaining ground; there has been a revival in the philosophy of religion; the sociology of religion after waiting a long time on the side-lines is now growing fast; and christian ethics (or moral and social theology) is more and more improving its position; only the psychology of religion is lagging as a university study, though a confusing proliferation of extra-university courses is developing. The problem immediately arises, how to fit these studies in to the tradition theological course? There is no question of the basic position of biblical studies in Christian theology. In the last resort all the rest of us depend upon what our colleagues in the biblical field are doing. But we are bound to ask them for a radical re-consideration of the amount of time they require, and of what they consider necessary to teach, and how they are going to teach it, as compared with the situation when they could take the majority of the time available. This is particularly painful for them when the decline of classics in the schools has made it impossible for them to link theological to classical studies as in the past. The effort to keep up something like the old standards merely means that the student spends a lot of time on what to him seems dreary language study (unless he happens to be specially gifted in it). The easiest policy would be to lengthen the course, but for economic reasons, if no other, it is not open to us. There is no escape from re-thinking course requirements and the distribution of time.

All this pre-supposes theological study as continuing broadly within a Christian context, which is natural and right in this country with its Christian tradition, though other options should be and are available, as in the growth of degrees in religious studies. Another religion could be taken as the core and the course built up from that. A phenomenological study of religion is possible, historical and comparative, though the problem of selection would be acute. Or a start could be made from the psychological or sociological study of religions, or a particular one, and the course developed from there. Ideally one would like to see the last carried out jointly by faculties (or departments) of theology and social studies, with sufficient cross-fertilization for the methods and assumptions of the one to be under scrutiny by the other. One would like to see, for instance, the whole question of ideology in human thinking tackled by both. Whether this is possible depends partly on time-table difficulties but more than anything else on the interests and outlook of the academic staff involved. Theology can no longer command, even if she wished to. But theologians should be eager to co-operate in the university with any who will co-operate with them, and not try to insulate themselves from their colleagues in other disciplines in a corner where they are invulnerable. They may, however, find those colleagues so imbued with positivist assumptions as to be unwilling to co-operate with them. In that case nothing can be done until the personnel changes.

It is in this broad context that moral, social and pastoral theology must find its place. Whether and how far it moves outside the Christian context depends entirely on local circum-stances. I assume for present purposes that it does move within the Christian context. In the first instance its task is not to prescribe detailed answers to specific questions but to clarify the nature of what is claimed to be an authoritative moral vision, to show how it has been worked out in practice, and the prob-lems that have arisen in doing so, and then to clarify the best method of doing it. It is more concerned with a 'style' of life than principles from which detailed answers can be deduced. For instance, a main issue for us today is what Christian style of life is appropriate to a relatively affluent society as compared with one of relative scarcity which has been the background of Christian thinking in the past. We have not got far with it yet.

To carry on this task requires systematic study, both historical and contemporary. The problem of being empirically *au fait* with relevant data is almost overwhelming in a time of rapid change. It is like a hen trying to lay an egg on a moving staircase. It can only be done co-operatively, and much of it in group work, drawing upon a range of practical and theoretical knowledge. There are a whole series of fringes. Concerning all of them the theologian must make his contribution, but must also realize he can do little or nothing by himself. In isolation he is lost.

We have some examples of such work which can be quoted. Take the Board of Social Responsibility of the Church of England and its predecessor. There have been a whole series of group reports coming from them. *The Family in Contemporary Society* of 1958 has become a classic (and unfortunately is not kept in print). The group had the full-time services of a qualified econ-omist for one year. Its report was so well argued, particularly on the subject of family planning and responsible parenthood, that it enabled the bishops at the Lambeth Conference in 1958 themselves to achieve a notable statement on the matter, a breakthrough which was quickly followed the next year in a Consultation called by the World Council of Churches. *Ought Suicide to be a Crime?* followed in 1959; it exposed the unconvincingness of many traditional arguments and influenced subsequent legislation on the subject. In 1962 there was a report on *Sterilization*, bringing to bear new information on an old issue, largely at the request of the Church of India, Burma and Ceylon. The problems of the traditional respect for life in medical ethics in the light of new techniques was the subject of the report *Decisions about Life and Death*, 1965. Next year one on *Abortion* has proved invaluable in view of continuing public discussion and legislation. It is a pity that it has not been more heeded. *Putting Asunder* (1966), an attempt to arrive at a more satisfactory public divorce law, has had a lot of influence. This had a slightly different provenance which does not affect the point being made. During roughly the same period the British Council of Churches has issued a series of reports on war, and the issues of defence and armaments in the light of the current British situation, and also on other questions, notably race. The Christian Citizenship Department of the Methodist Church has similarly issued reports, the latest being one on *Censorship* 1971. The World Council of Churches has also produced several, notably *Experiments with Man* (1968) in the light of developments in molecular biology. This is only a selection of examples quoted for our encouragement.

Even the most cursory looking ahead can see some fringe problems which demand co-operative work; one thinks of 'genetical engineering', of the range of issues involved in development, technology and social justice; of nature conservation and pollution; of rebellion, revolution and violence; and of the general issues summed up in the barbarous and misleading term 'futurology', as mankind more and more consciously organizes itself towards the year 2000. (The term is misleading because it suggests a science as a basis of prediction which does not exist.)

One may reasonably hope by co-operative work to achieve enough agreement to give general guidance for Christian action. It is unlikely that specific and detailed conclusions can often be arrived at; there are too many empirical hazards in assessing the factors at work, the trends, and the likely consequences of actions. But this middle ground between the general and the very specific is of immense importance in helping Christian thinking to be clear and effective. It is often called the level of 'middle axioms'.[5]

These benefits can flow from a situation on the fringe, the boundary, the borderline, or the margin. It is not a place of security or of perfection. It is a place of risk. The impossibility of merely repeating the old destroys the security of sticking by the familiar. If in the end it is reiterated, it has had to be thought out anew. If new positions are called for, it is an arduous task to arrive at them. Either course involves the risk of error. But there is no possibility of avoiding error. We live by faith and not by sight. Christians of all people should be alert to this. Finally we stand neither at a fringe nor at a boundary but at a limit. This is the limit constituted by God himself, where the man made in the image of God stands before his creator. To the Christian this is not a place of dread but of ultimate security in Christ; and this limit gives him all the freedom of response that a life of sonship requires.

5

From the Bible to the Modern World: A Problem for Ecumenical Ethics

I

The question of the nature and authority of the Bible has inevitably been one of the main preoccupations of study in the ecumenical movement, because it was one of the main causes of confessional divisions in the past. Part of this study has just as inevitably been concerned with ethics, particularly social ethics, for disagreements between Christians on these questions have been equally divisive. Richard Niebuhr's valuable study *Christ and Culture*[1] has shown how five characteristic attitudes have continually been taken on the relation of the two, all drawing on the same biblical material, and these have frequently been a cause of strife within and between confessions.

Any consideration of a normative ethic must deal with the two questions of (*i*) the right *motive* for action, and (*ii*) how to achieve the right *content* in action in particular circumstances. Christian ethics has to deal with these two questions as has any other normative ethic: therefore what relation the Bible, among other possible sources of help within the Christian tradition, has to them is bound to be raised. Indeed, the influence of the Bible has been so pervasive, and frequently so restrictive, that I was tempted to call this lecture 'The Tyranny of the Black Book', borrowing a phrase referring to the Bible of the Welsh poet R. S. Thomas.

As part of a study of the authority of the Bible in general (of which the ethical aspect is a part) we recall that from its beginnings in the early decades of this century the ecumenical movement was heir to the historico-critical study of the Bible, which by then had had more than a century to get established, and was universally accepted in those circles which were prepared to take ecumenism seriously. This had shattered the belief in the unity of scripture and the rightness of it being seen within a framework of dogmatic theology, which had been the traditional position in all the different confessions. Since then the ecumenical movement has lived through the period of biblical theology. Its waxing was heralded by Karl Barth's *Römerbrief* in 1918, and its demise registered by Ernst Käsemann's speech at the Fourth World Conference on Faith and Order at Montreal in 1963; and its period of greatest flourishing could perhaps be said to be roughly the years 1935–55. As is well known, it attempted not to repudiate the gains of historico-critical study but, presuming them, to arrive at a synthesis called biblical theology, and in a sense to recover a more sophisticated version of the old position. The collapse of this has brought back the old vexing questions. I would not be thought to suggest that all has been a waste of time. Far from it. It would have been worse if we had never set out on the journey. As in the history of the Christian doctrine, the exploration of what turn out to be blind alleys illuminates the ongoing task of the church. This is the continued reflection in new situations on the significance of her doctrinal and ethical inheritance from the past, the Bible being a major part of it.

Until recently the Roman Catholic Church played no part in this. In 1893 Leo XIII in his encyclical *Providentissimus Deus* condemned the critical study of the scriptures; and the condemnation of Modernism in the encyclical of Pius X, *Pascendi dominici gregis* of 1907, was followed by the anti-Modernist oath of 1910 which contained an explicit repudiation of biblical criticism. Fruitful biblical study practically ceased in the Roman Catholic Church until the encyclical of Pius XII in 1943 *Divino afflante spiritu* encouraged it again. Since then scholars of that church have rapidly appropriated the pioneering work of others and are now in the forefront of biblical studies. Their work has had profound effects in Roman Catholic moral theology in the last fifteen or twenty years, which had grown remote from the Bible. But it was still some time before Roman Catholics could make a contribution to ecumenical studies. Pius XI in his encyclical *Mortalium Animus* in 1928 forbade Roman Catholics to give ecumenism encouragement or support, a prohibition which was only slightly modified by an Instruction from the Sacred Office in 1949. It was not until the Second Vatican Council of 1962–5 that the breakthrough came with the Decree of the Council *De Ecumenismo*. Since then Roman Catholic scholars have been co-operating fully in ecumenical studies, however cautious has been the approach of their church to ecumenical institutions. With respect to the place of the Bible there is a certain irony in the fact that the Roman Catholic Church is becoming very biblically orientated just at the time when other confessions which have been so are finding themselves forced once more to raise queries about the Bible in view of the breakdown of biblical theology. There is a danger that each may repeat the mistakes of the other. But if the ecumenical movement does maintain its momentum, something which is much to be hoped but cannot be assumed, the prospects of scholars of all confessions working together on the use of the Bible in the modern world are exciting indeed.

II

The ecumenical movement became official with the first Assembly of the World Council of Churches at Amsterdam in 1948. Just prior to this two ecumenical study conferences were held on the theme 'Biblical Authority for the Church's Social and Political Message To-day'; one in London in August 1946 and the other at the new Ecumenical Institute, Bossey, near Geneva in January 1947. The work of these conferences was written up in a fairly substantial mimeographed book, *From the Bible to the Modern World* (1947), from which I have taken the title of this lecture. I do not want to dwell upon it now, except to note that it says that the growth of biblical theology, with its two-fold affirmation of the Bible as God's word and Jesus Christ as Lord, has meant that tension between liberals and conservatives in attitudes to the Bible has eased, but that many problems arise in relating it to modern society. More important is the book *Biblical Authority for Today*,[2] edited by Alan Richardson and Wolfgang Schweitzer, which contains articles on different confessional positions on 'The Authority of the Bible', on 'Principles of Interpretation', and on 'Specific Applications'. The preface makes large claims to agreement on the meaning and relevance of specific passages. The most important section, however, is an agreed statement on 'Guiding Principles for Interpretation of the Bible'[3] as accepted by an Ecumenical Study Conference at Oxford in 1949. (It should be recalled that at this stage no

Roman Catholics could take part and so none was involved in this acceptance.) It has four sections:

1. *The necessary theological presuppositions of biblical interpretation*

Some would query whether talking of *theological* presupposi-tions does not already beg a fundamental question and presup-pose a greater unity in the Bible than exists, thus reflecting all too clearly the mistake of the approach of biblical theology. I shall return to this point. I refer now only to the last half sentence of the section which says 'any teaching that clearly contradicts *the* [my italics] Biblical position cannot be accepted as Christian'.[4] This certainly assumes a unity of biblical positions which few could maintain today.

2. *The interpretation of specific passages*

This deals with questions of original meaning and context, presupposing historico-critical methods of study, and ends with the need to 'see and expound the passage in the light of the whole scope of *Heilesgeschichte*', a favourite term of biblical theology.

3. *The discovery of the biblical teaching on a specific social or political issue*

This starts by saying that 'one must begin with a direct study of the biblical text in relation to a given problem; otherwise the general principles which we establish will reflect more the pre-suppositions of our own time than the message of the Bible'.[5] This seems to presuppose a relation of the biblical text to a given modern problem which is really the main question. Where the problem dealt with is the same today, for example divorce, it is the nature of the text that needs exploring; and in the case of the many modern problems which are not dealt with in the Bible, 'factory farming' to take one instance at random, it is the relation between them and the Bible which needs establishing. Later points in this section include wise remarks about the need for care in assessing texts in too facile a manner, lest the Bible be 'made to present a united witness on a topic which in fact it does not do'; and it ends with the valuable point that 'the scriptural teaching of the two ages has an important bearing upon the way in which a specific social or political issue is to be interpreted'.

4. *The application of the biblical message to the modern world*

This says that 'we must discover the degree to which our particular situation is similar to that which the Bible presents. It must be remembered that absolute identity of situation is never found, and therefore the problem of adaptation becomes acute'.[6] It adds that in applying the biblical message to our day all kinds of relativizing personal, cultural and confessional factors will cause interpreters to diverge, but that within the joint study of the ecumenical movement many of these presuppositions, some of them largely unconscious, are brought to the judgment of scripture, and the living word of God is heard.

These and other biblical issues have been studied with renewed vigour in the Faith and Order movement of the World Council of Churches since its Montreal Conference in 1963, through its Bristol one in 1967 to its one at Louvain in 1971.[7] The Dutch theologian of the Bible, Dr Ellen Flesseman-van Leer, gives a valuable report on this in an article 'Biblical Interpretation in the World Council of Churches' which was published in the WCC's quarterly, *Study Encounter*.[8] She is very critical of the 'Guiding Principles' on the grounds that they are christocentric, harmonizing and unhistorical. I think she is too critical. It is interesting how scholarship in theology, as in other disciplines, tends to proceed by a 'swing of the pendulum' motion, so that positions most criticized in one generation are those held a generation before, and it takes some time before a more adequate appraisal of them can be made. The same is often the case with great contemporary literary figures, whose reputation sinks rapidly after their death and then in due course recovers. In this case I was never an advocate of biblical theology, though I was influenced by it. I think that there is useful material embedded in the 'Guiding Principles', as I have indicated, and I shall return to it later.

However, Dr Flesseman-van Leer's main point is a strong one. It is that a major problem to be faced is how to bridge the gap between the point in time of the biblical writing and today. This is the question of hermeneutics, a term which was not in our vocabulary fifteen years ago but is now pervasive. The problem of hermeneutics is two fold. (*i*) To clarify what the author meant to say in his time and situation, or exegesis; with this we are familiar. (*ii*) To clarify how it can be expressed and communicated today, for to translate from one period or one idiom to another is to make a fresh proclamation; this is a fundamental linguistic and philosophical achievement to the hazards of which we have recently become much more alert. Biblical theology often emphasized the gap between man and God; yet the gap between then and now is just as great. Historical imagination, if it does its work thoroughly, may increase this second gap, as Albert Schweitzer said so forcefully early this century of the quest for the historical Jesus:

> It set out believing that when it had found him it would bring him straight into our time as Teacher and Saviour. It loosed the bands by which we had been riveted for centuries to the stony rocks of ecclesiastical doctrine, and rejoiced to see life and movement coming into the figure once more, and the historical Jesus advancing, it seemed to meet it. But he does not stay; he passes by our time and returns to his own. What surprised and dismayed the theology of the last forty years was that, despite all forced and arbitrary interpretations, it could not keep him in our time, but had to let him go. He returned to his own time, not owing to the application of any historical ingenuity, but by the same inevitable necessity by which the liberated pendulum returns to its original position.[9]

This again seems to me to be an overstatement of an important point. In some respects Jesus' outlook is seen firmly rooted in the first-century thought forms which cannot be easily translated into the twentieth century; in other respects not. This is where hermeneutics has its double task, not just to take us back to the text, or behind the text, but also from the text forwards. For, as in the case of any literary work of a poet or novelist, we are not concerned merely with the private intention of the author but with what he actually wrote, and what imaginative reflection on it within a community which draws sustenance from it may come to apprehend through it. We shall do this the more adequately the more we are open to the whole range of human experience, and of contemporary culture. Modern translations of the Bible illustrate this point very well. Of course their authors need to be expert in the linguistic disciplines of the original biblical languages. But that is only half the requirement. They need to be equally sensitive to the subtleties of the modern language into which they translate; that is to say they must be persons of wise cultural sensibilities. It is precisely here that the problems with modern translation mainly arise. Another way of putting the point is one insisted upon by Leonard Hodgson in his Gifford Lectures of 1955–7, *For Faith and Freedom*, when he says that a genuine historical investigation should lead to the question 'What must the truth have been and be if that is how it looked to men who thought and wrote like that.' He adds, 'But theology is bedevilled by the illusion that somewhere, sometime, someone really knew the full truth and that what we have to do is to study what he said or wrote, find out what he meant by it, and get back to it.' He criticizes the assumption that 'somewhere at some time it is possible to have a finally satisfactory statement of the truth'; rather 'God alone knows all the truth, and in this space-time universe is communicating it to us human beings as our growing minds grow in ability to receive it.'[10] Leaving aside that the adjective 'growing' applied to our minds is somewhat confident (technical know-how grows but in more fundamental matters minds may become darkened), the general drift of Hodgson's remarks seems cogent, and well suited to our task of considering the move from the Bible to the modern world with special reference to ethics.

One can say of these recent Faith and Order studies what Dr Flesseman-van Leer says[11] in particular of the Louvain Report, that they break through the 'stiff and static quality, which marks so many traditional concepts, thus making them more flexible and relative'. The Bristol one on 'The significance of the Hermeneutical Problem for the Ecumenical Movement' dealt with the first of the two hermeneutical tasks, scientific exegesis, and emphasized the diversity in scripture, the danger of easy harmonization, and elaborated Bultmann's concept of the element of 'pre-understanding' (*Vorverständnis*) which one inevitably brings to a study of the text. Bultmann confines this to the existentialist analysis of human existence, but this is too constricting. The important point to realize is that neither the person nor the community within which the person studies the biblical text is a *tabula rasa*, and that without their pre-understanding it would not be possible to proceed.

The Louvain report on 'The Authority of Scripture' again stressed the diversity within scripture, that there are several possible centres of interpretation of the Old Testament, and varying interpretations of God's redeeming act in Christ in the New Testament. Then in connection with the second task of hermeneutics – that of moving from the original text to the present situation – it spoke of 'a situation – conditional hermeneutical perspective'. That is to say that if the Bible is to be understood in our present situation, our understanding of that situation and our definition of the problem on which we want light to be thrown by the Bible are indispensable factors in receiving insights.

So much for World Council of Churches' studies. From these I draw three conclusions:

1. The Bible and the church must go together. Setting one against the other has been a disastrous consequence of Protestant-Catholic divisions. Confessions which emphasize *sola scriptura* must come to terms with this. Some scholars have indeed regarded both Bible and church as encumbrances. They regard the church as an institutional block to the living of Christian faith and life (that was the reason Charles Davis left the Roman Catholic Church), and they consider the creation of a canon of holy scripture as a failure of nerve on the part of the church. Such an anti-institutional attitude tends to be popular today. But both theologically and sociologically I would say that church and Bible are inevitable; the mistake has been to think of them both in too narrow and rigid terms. The church will continually read and reflect on the Bible as a decisive element in her own tradition. But she must not merely let the Bible question her, as biblical theology said; she must, from her own time-bound situations (to use a term of Karl Barth), address questions to the Bible.

2. The central significance of Jesus Christ is the key to understanding the Bible. This involves his relation to the Old Testament witness to the God first of Israel and then of all people, and to the new community which arose as a result of his mission and out of which the New Testament came. That the Bible correctly witnesses to the centrality of Christ is a presupposition of Christian faith, but to go further into that is not our present concern. What exactly that witness is remains a matter of continued reflection within the church, and this will include the using of all relevant scholarly skills.[12]

3. There is no direct route from the Bible to particular ethical decisions. What the Bible does is to provide a basic orientation, or stance, or vision of goodness which we bring alongside particular situations whose empirical nature we have to investigate. In this task imagination and empirical accuracy are related to one another. If we ask ourselves 'what is this situation about which we are ethically concerned?', it is true that there will be 'brute facts' which we need to know, and access to which Christians have no special privilege. It is also true that if we

have sensitive imaginations we shall see aspects of the situation to which otherwise we would be blind, and this may lead us to weigh the brute facts at different levels of significance from what otherwise we would have done. That is why moral judgment is an art. By continued sharing in the basic orientation, stance or vision of goodness focused in Jesus Christ, to which the Bible bears witness (which in practice means appropriating them within the Christian community), we may develop habits, or virtues, or a character which leads us to respond more readily and at deeper levels to that vision. The Bible in the church can do that for us, but it cannot provide by itself either unexceptionable moral rules, or detailed decisions, or middle axioms (half way between these two). There is often talk of 'Christian' or 'biblical' principles but it is generally imprecise. If it is meant that a general orientation is suggested by the biblical witness to Christ, this is so. 'Respect for persons' is one such; it is prominent in much Christian social ethics; for instance, in the teaching of William Temple. Within the overall respect for persons a particular concern for the disadvantaged and poor is often mentioned; and within the category of disadvantaged a concern for women. All of this seems cogent. When these general orientations come to be expressed in action, certain principles or rules may well develop, on the basis of experience in the course of Christian history, but they do not proceed directly from the Bible. In any case the question will always arise as to whether in a particular situation the rule will apply or not. That is to say that a basic question in moral philosophy, whether to proceed by a deontological or teleological route in any particular moral case, is one that the Christian has also to face. And any halfway 'middle axiom', or any detailed ethical conclusion, must involve some consideration of empirical evidence arising from the present situation and cannot be derived from the Bible direct.[13] This means that we must be prepared to use the ethical material in the Bible in a flexible way; but with a flexibility controlled by sound standards of scholarship, operating within the presuppositions I have mentioned and aware of their significance for the use of the Bible.

III

I turn now to give five examples of problems in the modern use of ethical material from the Bible:

1. *Eschatology as the key to New Testament ethics*

It seems clear from New Testament studies that are so numerous and so familiar that it is not necessary to specify them in detail, that the key concept in Jesus' mission and message was that of the kingdom or rule or reign of God, which he saw as having begun to exercise its authority in human life in his own activity. In this sense eschatological events, that is to say events of last or ultimate significance for humanity, were taking place through his own ministry. Much discussion has ensued as to how far his ministry focused on the present eschatological realization of these events and how far it heralded the imminent realization of them in the future. I think I represent a fair consensus when I say that the truth seems to be that Jesus regarded the kingdom as inaugurated in his own ministry but to be fully realized in the future (of which I shall have more to say shortly). The claim that the 'last' events of supreme significance, to which Old Testament hopes looked forward in their various ways, were taking place in his own ministry is, of course, a highly paradoxical one. So is the ethic which follows from it. Its most striking characteristic is that it is non-reciprocal. Whereas an everyday ethic operates on roughly a 'do as you would be done by' basis, and depends on it being reciprocated, so that we do good turns to those who do good turns to us, Jesus explicitly differentiates his teaching from that. His ethic, for instance, requires the forgiveness of those who injure us not seven times (which is as much as the disciples think is humanly possible) but four hundred and ninety times; thereby he transfers the matter into an entirely different dimension. The reason for such a far-reaching demand is the fact that such is the way God deals with us (Matt. 5.43ff.; 18.21), of which the weather and his own ministry are signs. For the characteristic motive for behaviour is that of a joyful response to the graciousness of God in the past and in his own ministry in the present. 'Freely you received, freely give' (Matt. 10.8). I am, of course, well aware of another motive for behaviour found in the gospels, that of rewards and punishments, but it is not the most distinctive one, and since I cannot go into it now I confine myself to saying that the rewards Jesus has to offer can only be appreciated by those who follow for love's sake not the reward's sake.

It is because the eschatological last days have dawned that

Jesus' ethic is so unlike that of Torah, in his attitude to which he exhibited what can only be called an eschatological freedom which could both respect (Matt. 8.4) and on occasion flatly contradict it (Mark 7.19). More important, he moved in a different dimension altogether. Detailed rules, like those of the Torah, had no place in the dawn of the eschatological age. That is why preoccupation with such questions as whether Jesus was sympathetic to the Zealots, or his teaching on divorce, is irrelevant if the preoccupation arises from the belief that the answer will tell us whether a Christian is justified now in taking part in armed revolt against his own state authority, or what rules either church or state should enact now with respect to marriages which have broken down. That is to make too direct a link between the biblical text and a particular situation later. Such questions must be investigated in order to understand Jesus as accurately as possible. Also it is true that if it appeared plausible that he was submerged in the Zealot presuppositions in particular, or those of his milieu in general, it would profoundly affect the Christian faith, just as it would have done if it had been plausibly shown, as the Christ-myth school maintained at the turn of the century, that he never lived. But the more thoroughly the New Testament is studied the more the eschatological freedom of Jesus stands out, rooted in his situation as a Jew in first-century Palestine and in the history of his people, but transcending it by the very fact that he did not deal with the relativities of particular ethical decisions. Note, for instance, that he did not give a clear ruling on what to render to Caesar and what to God (Mark 12.17).

This leaves us with the basic task of working out the implications of an eschatological ethic in the ongoing situations of life. The New Testament gives us some very revealing examples of ways in which the church attempted this.

(a) The earliest arose out of a combination of eschatological awareness with an apocalyptic outlook which expected the inaugurated reign of God to be completed by an imminent *parousia*. Did Jesus share this expectation himself? I have been disposed to think he did. Then I find that Käsemann thinks he did not[14] and now I am not so sure. However, it is a question I must leave to the New Testament scholars to settle, and I do not think that an answer either way is directly relevant to the questions with which I am now concerned. But there is no doubt that the earliest Christians did. St Paul's answers to the six questions about marriage asked of him by the deputation sent from Corinth is conditioned by this apocalyptic expectation (I Cor. 7.29). The Christians of the early church in Jerusalem, if we follow what Luke tells us in the last verses of chapters 2 and 4 of Acts, pooled their capital and lived on it in a similar expectation and one which, when unrealized, led to their impoverishment and to St Paul's organization of a relief fund for them from his gentile churches. Ethical responses when this belief is held are in a sense improvised and *ad hoc*; no long term continuity is involved. The Letters to the Seven Churches in chapters 2 and 3 of Revelation are a further example; the sense of apocalyptic imminence is so strong and the situation of each particular church so occasional that we cannot now tell what it was.

(b) As this apocalyptic sense faded and time went on, the process of arriving at standard ethical guidance to deal with standard situations developed. Since the Christians had no civic power or responsibility it was with respect to domestic situations that this guidance developed; the need was to deal with ongoing problems of family and household relationships. That is why we find the household codes embedded in the later Pauline epistles, the pastoral epistles and I Peter (Col. 3.18–4.1; Eph. 5.12–6.9; I Peter 2.11–3.12 and 5.1–5; Titus 2.1–3.2; I Tim. 2.1–6.19). To my mind the treatment of them in Kenneth Kirk's *The Vision of God*, Lectures 2 and 3, is still the most satisfactory.[15] The problem was to deal with ongoing ethical problems without losing the eschatological freedom and newness characteristic of Jesus. It was for the most part only partially solved. Kirk differentiates three tendencies, codification, formalism and rigorism, examples of which can be found within the New Testament and spilling over into the writings of the apostolic fathers. The household codes in Colossians and Ephesians show signs of taking over a common morality, albeit with a Stoic flavour, and substituting Christian exemplars and motives. The pastoral epistles show signs of contentment with a more formally observed external ethic; the church has become an enclave of the world, respectful of the authorities and the social order. On the other hand, signs of an opposite and rigorist attitude are found in other later New Testament writings, for example in I John 5.16 and Heb. 6.4–6; 10.26–31; 12.16ff. In the way the teaching of Jesus is presented in chapters 5 to 7 of Matthew, the sermon on the mount shows signs of all these tendencies, and so does the teaching of St Paul in what we might call his middle period. Romans 12 shows great affinity with the sermon on the mount whilst Romans 13 retains more of the apocalyptic note. These examples show the freedom with which the church reflected on her traditions, the same freedom which we have seen to be necessary today.

(*c*) There is nothing wrong in codification provided the sense of eschatological renewal is not lost. The problem is to preserve it without the apocalyptic belief in an imminent *parousia* with which it had been associated from the earliest days of the church (whether in the mind of Jesus or not). The ethic of the Johannine literature is of great interest in this respect since it recovers the eschatology without the apocalypticism. It witnesses to a fundamental theological reappraisal having taken place by the end of the first century with the dropping of imminent apocalypticism. A trace remains in I John (2.18) but no more, and it is quite absent from the Fourth Gospel. The writer has reflected deeply on Jesus' eschatological ethic of *agape* and presents it in all its depth and rigour. It is true that something appears to be lost in that it is related to the fellow Christian rather than to the wider range of any man in need, as represented by the allegory of the sheep and the goats in Matthew 25, but this can be overstated since it is clear that it is all with an intention that goes outward, so that 'the world may believe' (John 17.21).

The Johannine ethic, however, does not cover the other half of the Christian ethical task, that of dealing with specific problems in an ongoing world. In discharging this it is vital to realize that the realization of *agape* is not a simple possibility in everyday life. Much of the wooden treatment of the Bible would have been avoided if this had been grasped. *Agape*, as taught and lived by Jesus, or as presented by St Paul in I Corinthians 13, which is a faithful reflection of it, represents a quality of life which discloses more depths the more you penetrate it; or fresh heights come into view as you scale the lower slopes. The more loving you become the more you find to draw you on. It is inexhaustible *in via*. But that does not mean that it is irrelevant. The efforts to explore its realization in practice in rules which may be codified is a necessary activity; otherwise we should be living all the time from moment to moment like an extempore speaker, and could never learn from experience. If the rules are wise it will be because they are seen to be what love requires. That is why St Thomas Aquinas' teaching on the just war is part of his treatment of charity.[16] But the richness, complexity and changes of human life and circumstances are such that an element of the provisional hangs over even the most solidly based rule, which in principle is open to revision simply because in the last resort *agape* cannot be exhaustively expressed.

This basic understanding of Christian ethics derived from the eschatologically significant ministry of Jesus, is not in essence hard to understand in the twentieth century. The first hermeneutical task of exegesis, making it clear in its context, is something which has been the basic concern of New Testament scholars. The road has been exciting and tortuous but there seems no reason to doubt that sufficient has been made clear as a basis for living. The second hermeneutical task of translating it into our situation does not appear too difficult as far as the essentials of the eschatological newness of *agape* is concerned. If the Johannine literature can present it without an apocalyptically imminent *parousia* so can we. Presented in this way it will remain relevant as long as time lasts. This does not necessarily mean that it will be easily received. Many may be hard of hearing. There may be extraneous obstacles to hearing. Anyone who is convinced that what is of eschatological significance cannot be in the past but must lie, if at all, in the future, cannot hear it. And the development of science and technology, which is always pushing the frontiers of knowledge into the future, leads many to assume that this is the model for every kind of knowledge. Nevertheless I see no reason in principle why the task of making the essence of the ethics of the New Testament intelligible today cannot be accomplished.

In saying this I must partly take issue with a very recent and able discussion, *Ethics in the New Testament*[17] by Jack T. Sanders of the University of Oregon. He maintains that one cannot live continuously under the command of love, without eschatological sanctions (p. 39), and that to maintain the language of imminent eschatology when it ceases to be imminent leads to an impossible ethical situation (p. 48). Knowing that my life is running out is not the same as knowing that the *parousia* is imminent (p. 16). The teaching of the sermon on the mount is preposterous without the *parousia* (p. 45). The household codes represent an insignificant popular morality which is completely worthless for Christian ethics (p. 75). The ethic of the Johannine literature is that of the new fundamentalism; according to it all you can do for your neighbour is to bring him back to Christ

(p. 100). The Johannine ethic is morally bankrupt. These judgments are, of course, buttressed by scholarly argument and not just thrown at the reader as *obiter dicta*. My own reaction to them will I hope be to some extent evident from what I have said earlier. I think once more they are an overstatement of a case. If one wants to move directly from these particular ethical stances of the New Testament to the modern world the criticism of them is to a large extent valid. Almost the only valuable teaching that Sanders finds is James 2.15ff., which calls for a human response to a basic human need (p. 126), whether the needy one is a Christian or not. I think he overlooks the fact that the *content* of Christian ethics may overlap with conventional ethics to a considerable extent, as it is worked out in particular situations, particularly collective ones; but it will always be set in a new, non-reciprocal, transcendent dimension. To bring this out is, in fact, Sanders' intention, for at the end of his admittedly negative book he asks, 'Can theologians and philosophers reflect . . . on the validity of the concept of transcendent love and the implications of such a notion? Otherwise throw out the New Testament as an aid to ethics once and for all' (p. 129). If he had made a clearer distinction between eschatology and apocalyptic Sanders would not need to have written so negatively until almost the last page of his book.

2. *The abandonment of apocalyptic as a concept of ethical use to us*

It may seem paradoxical to suggest this when Käsemann has called it 'the mother of all Christian Theology',[18] even though theology soon moved away from mother's apron strings, for it did not outlast the collapse of the hope of the *parousia* and the start of the gentile mission. Moreover, apocalyptic has come into favour in some modern theology. Pannenberg views it as a revelation of universal history which can only be seen from its end, of which the resurrection of Jesus is proleptic. Moltmann stresses a hope and promise in the Christian faith which proclaims the future as unlimitedly new, with a radical discontinuity from the present.[19] There are in my judgment serious difficulties in these views. The more one emphasizes radical newness and discontinuity, the more useless it is in providing a guide to the present. Presumably not all that is radically new and discontinuous can necessarily be approved of, and if change itself is not a criterion, a basis for evaluating and guiding it must be found in what we already know, and this is based on our present understanding of the past. This is, in fact, explicit in the greatest Christian apocalyptic, Revelation, where the Lamb who was slain in the course of human history in the past is the key to the visions of the future. There are, however, other serious difficulties in apocalyptic thought which I can most concisely summarize in a quotation from what I have written elsewhere:

   (i) It has claimed too much knowledge of the future in God's intention, continually forecasting the date of the *parousia* and not being willing enough to live by faith.
  (ii) It has had a pessimistic view of history, assuming that things must get worse before Yahweh intervenes to sort out the mess and vindicate his faithful. History comes to a terminus not a *telos*.
 (iii) It has not attached much importance in any case to ongoing events in human history in view of the expected cataclysmic future, all of which is determined.
  (iv) Its hopes for an absolutely new future have been too discontinuous with the ongoing events in human history.
   (v) Believers have been too certain of their place in the new post-apocalyptic order, and too certain that it is an exclusive place. Apocalyptic literature is full of cries for vengeance, there is no hope of expectation or apparent desire that a sinner may change, or any sense of God's love for the sinner.[20]

In my judgment apocalyptic thought cannot be rendered intelligible or useful today by any process of hermeneutics, and it is useless to us theologically and ethically. Any ideas derived from it which do provide valid insights, such as belief that human history is working out within the scope of divine providence, despite the power of evil forces, and that providence extends beyond this terrestrial life of ours, is not peculiar to apocalyptic, and so we shall lose nothing by dispensing with it.

3. *The relation of problems of power and justice in human society to the eschatological reality of the inaugurated kingdom of God*

The fact that no clear link is made between the two in the teaching of Jesus has not created the difficulty in Christian history that might have been expected, because resort has been made to particular teachings in other New Testament writings (Romans 13.1–7 on the state being an obvious example), without allowing for their relative and conditioned character. Resort to the Old Testament has had an added defect, because the New Testament writings are at any rate responding to a new understanding of God through Jesus Christ, whereas those of the Old Testament are not, and yet have often been treated as though they were on the same plane. In the Old Testament God's power is seen first of all in history, especially in creating and then preserving his people. His power over nature was apprehended after this and as a partial corollary of it, and from this man's power over nature was derived, as developed for instance in the myth or parable of Genesis 1. In the New Testament God's bestowal of power is connected with the vastly deepened gift of the Spirit – who had spoken by the prophets, as the Nicene Creed says – in the eschatological age inaugurated by Jesus. And it is power expressed in a way as paradoxical as the non-reciprocal ethic (Mark 10.42–45) so that it can be mistaken for powerlessness. There are also angelic and demonic spirits, as part of the intellectual *mise en scène* of the first century, but since Jesus Christ is held to be superior to the angelic ones and to have dethroned the demonic ones, they need not concern us further. The important point is that there is no worked out concept of secular power for the service of men. This is because in the Old Testament a theocracy was assumed, and in the New Testament the church was so insignificant in the Roman Empire that the issue did not arise for it; and there were the imminent apocalyptic expectations held by most of the writers which made it in any case an irrelevant one. If the various texts on the subject of secular power are considered in their contexts and woven together in some sort of pattern it amounts to saying that when the state authority is neutral to the church it is to be firmly obeyed, and when it is hostile it is to be enduringly opposed. To try to follow this maxim today in situations as diverse as China, Pakistan, Spain, South Africa, Chile, Eire, Cuba (to make a random selection) is to show what a wooden and mistaken way of using scripture this would be; truly a tyranny of the Black Book.

Again, if we turn to the question of justice, the ethical teaching of Jesus is not of much direct help on a great number of issues which cannot be avoided. Indeed it appears to be anarchic and utterly indifferent to collective issues. It certainly does give a strong indication that God is 'biased' on the side of the poor and unprivileged, and the strain in the Old Testament which links wealth with divine approval is corrected by it. This bears on distributive justice; but there are many other issues, such as those concerned with corrective justice, which have to be faced. So it is not surprising that an immense literature has grown up on justice because of issues, inevitable in civil society, arising in this field. The 'justice tract' in traditional moral theology looms extremely large, so large that a student never gathers that it is all in the service of love. Yet it is too simple to say with Joseph Fletcher in his various works that justice is nothing but love distributed. That could only be so if *agape* was solely conceived in terms of what is done, to the exclusion of concern for the motive for which it is done; and also if we were concerned only with the quantity of *agape*, so to speak and not with its manner of distribution. Other theologians, like Nygren, have opposed love and justice.[21] Rather they must be related. There is no justice without an element of love, at least in the sense of affirming the other in his otherness as a person and not because of his function. There is also no love without justice, otherwise we have either sentimentality or egoism. Love presupposes justice; it can never require less than justice and never be a substitute for it (in the sense of 'acts of charity'), but it points to the inexhaustible creative love which transcends any particular responsive embodiment of it.

The New Testament doctrine of the two ages, developed in their own way by St Augustine with his two cities and Luther with his two realms or kingdoms, is the setting within which the ongoing problems of social ethics are best related to the eschatological ethics of love. They have sometimes been used, as has the Bible, in a wooden way which makes a rigid and inflexible gulf between the two. But there is no necessity for this, and there are plenty of indications of a more flexible way of relating them which we cannot discuss now.

4. Care in the use of the Old Testament as a model

This illustrates the dangers of not using the concept of the two kingdoms, and arises from the desire to make too direct a link between the Bible and some specific decision in the contemporary world. This constantly crops up in the most respectable theologies. Karl Barth frequently makes these sudden darts from a biblical text to a specific conclusion. One of the most well known is his statement that because Jesus Christ is the light of the world the church must be the sworn enemy of all secret diplomacy.[22] It would be illuminating to work through ecumenical documents to see how often a similar thing is done and with what effect. I have occasionally noted instances, but never worked at it systematically. I suspect that it is particularly a legacy of Calvinist theology. The examples I have in mind at the moment both concern the Old Testament. Theologies of liberation and revolution are making much of the Exodus saga as the model for discussing God's activity in history today. But how by itself does it enable one to judge between the various changes which are dramatic and discontinuous? Change itself is not a criterion; and some of it presumably is *counter*-revolutionary. How do we discriminate? Moreover what of the settlement? What of those who were disturbed and possibly displaced in order that the people of Israel might settle? And what of the exile? Why is that central event in Old Testament history not made a key model of interpretation? It all savours of covering subjectivity in using the Bible with a mask of objectivity. The root of the matter is that in the Old Testament there is only one kingdom, which is also the people of God, the church; it is both church and state. History is interpreted from the point of view of its choice, guidance and disciplining by Yahweh. The people of God in the New Testament has broken the bounds of the one kingdom and become in principle universal. There are now two kingdoms, that of the people of God and that of the terrestrial state, and the Christian lives in the two at once. It is as illegitimate to transfer models from the Old Testament to secular kingdoms (or to the church) now as it was to regard Tudor monarchs as Godly Princes on the model of King David. In particular it imparts a dangerous messianic tone to contemporary Christian attitudes which exacerbates divisions and clouds judgments.

A different case is the use of the Genesis creation saga in connection with recent environmental controversies concerned with the pollution of earth, water and atmosphere, the wanton use of irreplaceable natural resources, and damage to the ecological balance of nature. I think there has been much exaggeration on all three points, but there is some truth in the charges. The Judeao-Christian tradition has been attacked for preaching a crude domination of man over nature on the basis of Genesis 1. The attack flatters the influence of that tradition in any case but, be that as it may, Christian theologians have come to the defence of their tradition and found meanings in Genesis 1 which fit the policies the critics advocate. But why do we feel obliged to base our teaching on Genesis 1? We are in danger of imitating Karl Barth, who found an enormous amount ostensi-

bly in Genesis 1.21 on sexuality in man and woman which no
one had ever seen there before, and which in fact came from a
whole range of aids to theological reflection, not least secular
knowledge developed in the course of time in the human
sciences.[23] It is the tyranny of the Black Book again. We need
all these resources to deal with the problem of man and nature,
just as we do to deal with man and the state.

5. *Attention to the relative and conditioned element in the New
   Testament teaching on specific ethical problems*

This point has perhaps been sufficiently made by now, so
that a brief mention in conclusion is all that is called for. The
teaching may be conditioned by the total social, economic, political and cultural situation of the first century, and in that sense
be 'time bound', to repeat Karl Barth's useful term. We can see
that it would have been impossible for St Paul to stand outside
the institution of slavery and conceive it not being there, that
is to say as an institution that might be abolished. Similarly he
could not have known that there are some five per cent of each
sex who are by 'nature' homosexual. However, the teaching
may also be limited because it is imperfectly Christian. In certain
places St Paul writes like a male Jew of the first century with
respect to women (I Cor. 11.2–6; 14.34–36). Not every corner of
his mind had seen the implications of his new faith. There is
nothing to be surprised at in this. His central affirmations seem
wholly in line with the eschatological newness of Jesus' ethic,
and this is the main thing. It only causes trouble if we use his
teaching in a wooden way.

An instance of a different kind is that of food offered to idols
where he is in a sense 'too Christian' in resolving the dilemma
(I Cor. 8. ff.: cf. Rom. 14). It will be recalled that he urges three
principles on a matter of secondary importance, as he held this
to be: (1) Follow conscience. (2) Do not upset a weaker brother.
(3) If these two come into conflict, the second should have
preference over the first. It seems very Christian, but as it stands
it hands the church over to those who suffer from what moral
theologians call a scrupulous conscience (a well-known phenomenon to anyone who gives spiritual guidance), and if consist-
ently followed would lead to a frighteningly restricted and timid
way of church life.

A final example is the subordinationist ethic in the Pastoral
Epistles, where in the case of husbands and wives, masters and

slaves, fathers and children, only the party who is called upon to show obedience is dealt with. This is one of the influences which have produced an excessive emphasis on obedience in the history of Christian ethics and it has given a handle to Marxist critics of it. The emphasis in it on patience and submission is indeed serious in an age which calls out for an ethic of responsibility.

We have travelled a considerable distance from the heights of general issues of hermeneutics to details in the pastoral epistles. We are in danger of seeming to end with a whisper and not a bang. However, the journey has been in aid of liberating us from a tyranny based on the Bible to an affirmation of the Bible as a continued source of renewal, when drawn upon in the church by those who are sensitive to the needs of their own day and wish to press on, as they are bound with others in the bundle of humanity, to their full stature in Christ.

6

Thirty-five Years Later, 1941-76 – William Temple's Christianity and Social Order

This book originally appeared as a Penguin Special in 1942, but the Preface was dated 15 November, 1941, when William Temple was still Archbishop of York. By April of the next year he had become Archbishop of Canterbury. In May the book was reprinted and again in August. Soon it had sold well over 150,000 copies. There were further reprints, and in 1956 it was issued as a Pelican, but it has been unobtainable for a number of years. My own copy of the original edition has nearly disintegrated with use and has been preserved from total collapse by being kept in one of the Penguin cellophane covers. A reissue of it deserves our unqualified welcome, both because it is a key piece of writing in British Christianity this century, and also because no book has as yet replaced it. One is urgently needed, but in its absence we cannot do better than make a serious re-appraisal of *Christianity and Social Order*. I will attempt first to locate the book in the national context of 1941 and of Temple's own outlook, secondly to draw attention to some salient points in the book, thirdly to reflect on what has happened since 1941, with the aim of suggesting what in its approach is of continuing significance.

I

There is little doubt that *Christianity and Social Order* represents a summary of views which Temple had held in general, if not in detail, for most of his working life, but the occasion of its publication was a growing sense in the country at large that a time of war should be a time of reformation; that the enormous effort to overcome the monstrous evil of Nazism, which taxed the British to the uttermost, should be followed – and the British did not allow themselves to entertain the idea that it might not be successful – by a 'new deal'. It was the time of the Beveridge Report with its call for a war against the five giants of want, disease, ignorance, squalor and idleness. In 1943 Temple was to take the chair at a meeting addressed by Beveridge on these matters. It was a developing conviction in the country, which led to the victory of the Labour Party in the General Election of 1945, and the creation of the kind of 'welfare state' in which we still live. It is true that adumbrations of it go back to the Liberal victory at the 1905 election, and perhaps further, but few would deny that the years from 1945 were the decisive ones in its history. Temple's influence in this respect was powerful, as was recognized at the time. The Italian theologian Ernesto Buonauti writing in *La Nuova Europa* in 1945, held that the Archbishop's involvement in the Labour Movement diverted it from more revolutionary outlets. This was to over-simplify. Even if Morgan Phillips' remark that the Labour Movement owed more to Methodism than to Marx is added, it would still be an over-simplification. The point was better put by Denys Munby of Nuffield College, Oxford in *God and the Rich Society*,[1] when he describes *Christianity and Social Order* as 'one of the foundation piers of the Welfare State' (p. 157).

As far as Temple himself was concerned, the immediate context of the book was the Malvern Conference on 'The Life of the Church and the Order of Society', called by him in January 1941. This was stimulating but incoherent, in that the two main groups behind the organization of it did not agree in their diagnosis. One held that the main task was a frontal attack on current economic institutions in favour of common ownership, and the other that it was a theological critique, largely based on the doctrine of Natural Law, leading to economic institutions of a different kind from that advocated by any of the political parties. Even Temple's genius as a chairman could not bring coherence into the proceedings. It was in this same year that Temple was asked to write a companion Penguin volume to that by the Bishop of Chichester, G. K. A. Bell, on *Christianity and World Order* (1940). This book is the result. It is a conscious tract for the times, little longer than many pamphlets, and shorter than some, and yet covering a reasonable range of ground. Temple was only to return once more in print to this theme[2] before his death in 1944, and that was a supplement to the *Christian News Letter* of 29 December 1943 (subsequently reprinted as a pamphlet), on 'What Christians stand for in the Secular World'.

This present book was obviously and inevitably written in haste. There is a certain looseness in construction; for instance love and justice only make their appearance, and that a brief one, at the beginning of the chapter dealing with the Natural Order. There are also some incautious phrases, for instance that Calvinism was 'the mainspring of unrestricted enterprise and competition' (p. 55), but no useful purpose is served by a dissection of these now. Temple himself remarks (p. 76) that he found it hard to write about Christianity and social order without writing about everything else at the same time, and I have the same difficulty with this introduction. In the book Temple is consciously addressing a much wider public than usual in his books, and he wants (*i*) to vindicate the church's right and duty to 'intervene' on these issues, (*ii*) to show that it has something worthwhile to say, and (*iii*) to indicate clearly where the competence of the church ceases because the issues at that level involve technicalities where she has no special competence. It is for this reason that he separates most of his own particular proposals in an Appendix so that their merits could be assessed independently of his main argument. In my view he is successful in this separation, though he does not show sufficiently clearly how one proceeds from his basic foundations to his particular proposals. To do so would involve a discussion of what are sometimes known by the forbidding term of 'middle axioms', which lie behind what he says on p. 58 but are not explicitly referred to, though Temple is well aware of the problem and the term, as his introduction to the report of the Malvern Conference, *Malvern 1941*, makes clear.[3]

In brief, middle axioms are an attempt to proceed from the basic ethical stance deriving from a theological or philosophical world-view to the realm of the empirical by seeing if there is a consensus among those with *relevant experience* of the matter under discussion (both 'experts' and 'lay' folk) as to the broad moral issues raised, and the *general direction* in which social change should be worked for, without getting as far as *detailed* policies. These in most cases involve so many uncertainties of interpretation of evidence and estimates of possible consequences that it is most unlikely that a church as a whole, or any church group of any size, will agree. At this level Christian men and women must use their own judgment as workers and as citizens and, as Temple says, nine-tenths of effective Christian impact on the social order is to be found here and not in church pronouncements or the activities of ecclesiastical bodies or persons as such (p. 39). Nevertheless, middle axioms, if available, are a help to the formation of the mind of a Christian, and it is at this level that most of the ecumenical social study, which has been such a notable feature of the last fifty years, has for the most part operated.

It was his concern for the witness of the church as such which made Temple anxious to speak in the main body of the book not in a personal capacity, but to voice 'the main trend of Christian social teaching', to quote his Preface. He goes back to the Old Testament, to the Fathers, to St Thomas Aquinas and (less confidently) to the Reformers. He draws a great deal on R. H. Tawney's *Religion and the Rise of Capitalism* and on the symposium edited in 1913 by Bishop Charles Gore, *Property: its Duties and Rights*, both indispensable books still.[4] Tawney is among those to whom Temple expresses special thanks for commenting on the typescript, whilst J. M. Keynes read the galley proofs. Temple was haunted by the charge that it was improper for the church to 'interfere' in these matters, a charge which is still resurrected though with ever diminishing credibility. It remains true, however, that if the church supports established institutions it usually passes without comment; it is when she criticizes them that the charge of interference is heard. Keynes' reply is so interesting that it is worth quoting at length from F. A. Iremonger's biography, *William Temple*.[5]

> I should have thought that in Chapter 1 you understated your case. Along one line of origin at least, economics more properly called political economy is on the side of ethics. Marshall always used to insist that it was through ethics that he arrived at political economy and I would claim myself in this, as in other respects, to be a pupil of his. I should have thought that nearly all English economists in the tradition, apart from Ricardo, reached economics that way. There are practically no issues of policy as distinct from technique which do not involve ethical considerations. If this is emphasized, the right of the Church to interfere in what is essentially a branch of ethics becomes even more obvious.
>
> I should have thought again that you were understating your case in the third chapter, where you consider the past record of the Church in these matters. I should have supposed that it was a very recent heresy indeed to cut these matters out of its province. Are

you not going too far in suggesting that in the XVIII Century the Church accepted this limitation? I should have thought decidedly not. Leaving out the Scots, such as Hume and Adam Smith, and foreign residents in London, such as Mandeville and Cantillon, I can think of no one important in the development of politico-economic ideas, apart from Bentham, who was not a clergyman and in most cases a high dignitary of the Church. For example, Dean Swift interested himself in these matters. Bishop Fleetwood wrote the first scientific treatise on price and the theory of index numbers. Bishop Berkeley wrote some of the shrewdest essays in these subjects available in his time. Bishop Butler, although primarily of ethical importance, is not to be neglected in this field. Archdeacon Paley is of fundamental importance. The Reverend T. R. Malthus was the greatest economist writing in the XVIII Century after Adam Smith. I agree that unless one includes Laud there are not many Archbishops before yourself to be included in the list. But Archbishop Sumner's early work was on economics.

The point made by Keynes in his second paragraph is, of course, rather a different one from that which was Temple's concern. Keynes is referring to church dignitaries who made themselves masters of the subject of political economy as it was at the time, and actually made contributions to its development. That could not be said of Temple, and in any event it would be much more difficult to do in our age of much greater specialization. The Church of England has produced a handful of dignitaries trained in the natural sciences, but not a single one as yet trained in the social sciences. Temple was well informed on social issues but not in the field of economics and the social sciences as such. He was well aware of this, but it led him to take too seriously, especially in the last years of his life, some Christians who wrote so much and so critically about economics that people tended to assume that they must have been qualified in it and knew what they were talking about, and indeed that they were proposing pathbreaking advances in the subject. In fact none of them were qualified in it, and it led them and those who were influenced by them into many elementary errors. J. S. Carmichael and H. S. Goodwin in their *William Temple's Political Legacy*,[6] have no difficulty in showing some of Temple's errors, but the effect of their book is lessened by their naïve enthusiasm for liberalism in the narrow sense of *laissez-faire* and free competition; and the large number of competent economists who are also castigated by them leaves the reader feeling that Temple is in good company. The other book on the subject, *Social Concern in the Thought of William Temple*, by Robert Craig,[7] now Principal of the University College of Rhodesia, is in fact much stronger on the theological parts of his thought. A thorough survey of Temple's social teaching remains to be written.

The immediate roots of this social teaching were 1. Anglican incarnational theology from the time of F. D. Maurice through such thinkers as B. F. Westcott, Scott Holland and Charles Gore. 2. The ecumenical movement from its earliest beginnings in the COPEC Conference at Birmingham in 1924 (on politics, education and citizenship), of which Temple was chairman, and which was itself a British preparation for the 'Life and Work' Conference at Stockholm in 1925. He was prominent in the Oxford Conference on 'Church, Community and State' of 1937, and as a result came into touch with the social teaching of Emil Brunner, and especially Reinhold Niebuhr. 3. The Christendom Group in the Church of England, which at that time sponsored a journal of that name and an annual summer school of 'Christian Sociology' at Oxford; it particularly stressed the doctrine of Natural Law. Something needs to be said about each of these three:

1. The Anglican incarnational tradition in theology can conveniently be studied in Archbishop Ramsey's *From Gore to Temple*.[8] This is not the occasion to explore it in detail, nor to defend every aspect of it (for example from the charge that its doctrine of the Trinity verged on tritheism), nor to set much store by its confessional source. Its strength from our present concern is the forcible way it expressed a positive attitude to this world which must follow from the belief that 'the Word was made flesh', and brought a certain type of otherwordly pietist Christianity under critical scrutiny as verging on heresy. But we must not make too much of this. Richard Niebuhr's *Christ and Culture*[9] has convincingly shown that a 'Christ against Culture' attitude is one of five stances which have continually reappeared in the Christian church and which, whilst by no means adequate as a complete expression of the relation of Christianity to this world, at critical points is cogent and powerful. Also we need to remember that the key Christian doctrines link together, so that it is possible to reach a positive attitude to this world from all of them – creation, atonement, the church, the sacraments, the last things (to take a traditional division) – and not merely from the incarnation. Temple shows this in this book. A certain

blandness characterized the outlook of exponents of incarnational theology on the social order, which underplayed the
extent of the injustices, tensions and conflicts to be found in it.
Association with the ecumenical movement brought Temple
into touch with different strains, with theologians who objected
to the turning of the great themes of Christian theology arising
out of the events of Christ's life, death and resurrection into
social 'principles'. It was consciousness of this which led Temple
in his *Christian Newsletter* supplement to urge the necessity of
digging deeper theological foundations and of being content
with a less grandiose superstructure.

2. The influence of the incipient ecumenical movement was
as great as his influence on it. Reinhold Niebuhr is the key
figure here. Both he and Temple were equally prominent in the
Oxford Conference. The fourth of the six volumes of essays
published in 1938 on the theme of the Conference consists of
essays by seven theologians on the overall theme, 'Christian
Faith and the Common Life'. The third is by Temple (the fourth
by Niebuhr), and it represents what is in many ways a shorter,
trial run for *Christianity and Social Order*, and is a more taut and
powerful piece. Further, the influence of J. H. Oldham on Temple was considerable. He and W. A. Visser't Hooft edited a
preparatory volume for the Conference, *The Church and its Function in Society*, and his section is frequently reflected in this
present book.[10] So is the report of Section 3 of the Conference,
'Church, Community and State in Relation to the Economic
Order', which is probably the best of the six sectional reports
of the Conference, and the only one to be reprinted separately
in addition to its inclusion in the book of the proceedings of the
Conference, *The Churches Survey their Task*. It is one of the great
documents of Christian social ethics in this century, and considerably in advance, for example, of where the papal social
encyclicals had got by this time.

3. The element of the Natural Law tradition in Temple's
thought is even more difficult to deal with briefly than that of
the middle axioms. Christians are divided between those to
whom the term is familiar, even though their understanding of
it and its implications varies considerably, and those to whom
it is unknown or meaningless or theologically suspect. Indeed
one of the most cogent reflections on it known to me is the
sentence in the Introduction to the book, *Natural Law* by A. P.
d'Entrèves,[11] which refers to it as a notion 'laden with ambi-

guity even in the days when it was considered self-evident'. It is true that there has been some revival of Natural Law thinking, in the sense of holding that the making of moral judgments is 'natural' to man and part of what it distinctively means to be a human being. (This is what the Bible presupposes as much as it presupposes God.) It is also an affirmation that in making moral judgments men should not, and at their best do not, merely reflect their tastes and prejudices or those of their family, group or society, but are responding to what is the case, to a good and a right transcending their own. If someone makes the judgment 'Hitler was a bad man' he is stating what simply is the case.

But the doctrine of Natural Law has traditionally been used in a different way. It has been held that there is something fixed in 'nature' which man can perceive and to which he must conform, and which can be deduced from some general principle, or from the 'nature' of an act devoid of any particular human context. In this sense the doctrine has taken hard knocks recently. The heirs of those who used it most are now increasingly questioning it. Roman Catholic moral theology has undergone what can only be called a revolutionary change in the last twenty years. It is possible that this traditional use of the doctrine in the papal encyclical *Humanae Vitae* may be the last instance of it. Unfortunately it was this use that Temple adopted in his last years. It is reflected in this book, but on examination we can see that it is marginal to his argument. He tells us (p. 80) in a loosely written paragraph that the Natural Law or Order is discovered 'partly by observing generally accepted standards of judgment' (a statement which needs clarification, for one cannot tell whether he refers to the basic moral insight of man as such or to something more restricted), and 'partly by consideration of the proper function of whatever is the subject of enquiry', and that this is apprehended 'by a consideration of its own nature'. The chief conclusion he draws from this is that production exists for consumption and not *vice versa*. A first reflection is that it hardly needs a considerable theological apparatus to establish that goods and services are produced in order to be consumed. This is, of course, the lynch pin of the pure *laissez-faire* theory of capitalism, according to which the consumer is king. (It is not clear whether Temple realized this; I think not.) The practice, however, has been markedly different.[12] But apart from the difference between practice and theory, the principle is too simple to resolve the diverse conflicts in society. We have different interests as producers and consumers; and most of us have divided interests, in that over a small area we are producers and over a large one consumers; and as producers we may be consumers of raw materials or partially manufactured ones and producers of a finished product. Certainly consumers' interests need attention, and the recent moves by the Government and by a private body like the Consumers' Association to pay them more attention is to be welcomed, but it is too simple to say that in all conflicts of interest those of the consumers must carry most weight. To take one illustration, the National Coal Board has greatly reduced the number of persons engaged in coal mining since nationalization, and it has done it in a gradual and humane way without throwing individuals and communities on the scrap heap. However, it has only been possible because the rest of us have paid more for our coal than otherwise we would have done. And this was right.

Much of the concern lying behind the revived interest in Natural Law has now passed into ecumenical studies of the human (or the Humanum as it is often somewhat grandiloquently called), notably that headed by Canon David Jenkins from 1969 to 1973. It is interesting that the same concern has been reflected in folk songs in recent years. Man must respect nature, in the sense in which a sculptor must respect the nature of his material, but he is not a servant of it but a creative manipulator of it. He is challenged to achieve his full humanity in the world, to be truly human. We do not know all that he has in him to become. His potentialities will be further explored and achieved by negative judgments on the *status quo*, as we shall shortly see, and by acting on them as a basis for guiding social change; they are not developed by issuing *a priori* commands and prohibitions in the name of Natural Law as has so often been done in the past.

II

The central concern of Temple in this book is indeed that of the human. From basic Christian beliefs about God and man he draws what he calls primary and secondary principles. The primary one amounts to respect for persons, or rather the person-in-community, because of the inherently social character of man. With Jacques Maritain he draws a sharp distinction between the person and the individual, and influenced by them I have for a long time striven to banish the term individual from my Christian vocabulary. John Macmurray was later to expound this point in his own way in his Gifford Lectures of 1953 and 1954, *The Self as Agent*, and *Persons in Relation*, adumbrations of which had appeared in his *Freedom in the Modern World* in the decade before Temple's Penguin.[13] It has also, of course, an obvious relation to the thought of Kant, and indeed that of J. S. Mill, but it was not from these sources, nor the Oxford idealist philosophy of the late nineteenth century that Temple took it, but from Christian theology. Nevertheless, they helped, as other philosophies at different times have helped in other ways, Christians to draw from their faith insights which were latent but not fully realized.

In the course of his exposition, Temple skilfully brings in four rather different points. (*i*) The fact that respect for persons does not mean an idealized view of them, but seeing them as they are in their sin as well as their grandeur. This leads him to the most effective popular exposition of that doctrine confusingly called 'original sin' which I have ever read (p. 60). (*ii*) That the working of this principle in the social order is by a negative judgment on aspects of the *status quo*. I am sure this is right and it is important. We do not as Christians have a blueprint of an ideal social order; we are led to look at the present situation in the light of our Christian understanding of life and identify those aspects which particularly offend it, and say 'this won't do'. Then we have to get down to the detailed task of how to achieve change in the right direction. (*iii*) In dealing in politics with men as they are and not as they ought to be Temple arrives at a splendid 'realist' sentence. 'The art of Government in fact is the art of so ordering life that self-interest prompts what justice demands' (p. 65). The far-reaching implications of this are worth pondering. (*iv*) He brings out that the person is largely what he is because he is born into 'social units' which profoundly affect him, especially before he is consciously aware of them. He refers to the family and the nation. These are not 'deliberately manufactured structures' (p. 64) but 'the product of historical development'. Temple does not give any theological support for this, but he could have aptly done so by referring to the Reformation doctrine of the 'Orders of Creation'. I should have been happier if he had cited the state rather than the nation, for on examination the nation proves to be all too uncertain a concept to be given such basic status, whereas the political order of the state is fundamental. There are issues here too large to take up, but important because of the frequent identification in the modern world of Christianity with nationalism, and the fact that acquiescing in this or fostering it in each country is the easiest way for the church to be popular. The main point here is that the recognition of the basic importance of these 'social units' shows the folly of the argument frequently mooted as to whether Christians should be concerned with changing persons or changing structures. Both are equally important, for both influence the other for good or ill. In terms of this book we can see how important it is that structures should be humane and just because of their effect on persons.

The chapter on derivative principles mentions freedom, social fellowship and service. This leads Temple to stress the importance of intermediate groups, so that neither overall individualism nor collectivism is a satisfactory position. Here papal encyclicals are drawn on, from which the principle of subsidiarity might have been mentioned, that is to say that wider authorities should not take on what can adequately be discharged by more local ones.[14] In fact today we have the hard task of devising both wider and more local ones at the same time, from the Common Market to the neighbourhood. He also stresses the place of minorities, and mentions the role of Dissent in British life. He might well have referred in this connection to two short books by A. D. Lindsay, *The Essentials of Democracy* and *The Churches and Democracy*,[15] which have been neglected lately. A further point of political importance is the necessity of checking our narrower loyalties by our wider ones, where there is much to be said for which Temple had no space. He qualifies the point by an illustration which seems to me to go too far on the 'realist side'. 'If a man applies in the training of his children standards *not generally accepted in their circle* (my italics), and fails to bring the children themselves to accept them, the result is likely to be an alienation of the children, both from their father and from his standards' (p. 76). The problem is clear, but since one cannot know in advance whether one will bring one's children to challenge currently accepted standards, Temple's proviso seems to lead to a perpetual support of the *status quo*. (The kind of situation which Temple may well have had in mind is that of a parent who lives in social circles where it is customary to opt out of the state system of education and to pay the fees to send children to 'public' schools.)

The particular proposals Temple arrived at are not our special concern now. There is not all that difference between the last chapter, where they are more general, and the Appendix, where they are more detailed. Control of land use, and financial proposals come in the latter. Education figures in both. It is depressing in 1976 to be reminded by Temple in 1941 of what H. A. L. Fisher said in 1918 when introducing the Education Bill of that year, 'Every citizen under the age of eighteen should be regarded as primarily a subject of education, not primarily a factor in industry' (p. 102). For the rest, malnutrition is not what it was; the nation was better fed under war time rationing than it had been in peace time and we have not slipped back. We are also better clothed. Holidays with pay have been achieved; and family allowance after the first child (not the second as Temple advocates). Indeed our standard of living has doubled since this book was written. But housing remains a scandal; long-term unemployment is returning after we thought we had banished it, though the circumstances of those unemployed is much better than it was in the 1930s. Inequalities of wealth and power are still great. A. B. Atkinson's study, *On Equal Shares* (1972) indicated that 91% of the total personal wealth of the country is in the hands of the richest 10%, and 72% in that of 5% (p. 15). True, there are arguments about the calculations of these figures, and we now have a Royal Commission on the Distribution of Income and Wealth, but substantial inequality cannot be gainsaid. And as to power, the responsibility of the worker in industry is still slight. In short, social problems have proved more intractable than we expected. Temple's general attitude seems right. The root of the matter is that the very substance of his faith should make the Christian ask radical questions about his society, whereas throughout Christian history Christians have tended either to accept the political and economic structures as they found them unreflectively, or else explicitly identify them with the will of God.

III

What has happened since Temple's death which bears on this book? On the theological front I mention five points. (*i*) It is much more obvious than it was in 1941 that we live in a plural society. This makes his unguarded remark (p. 37) unfortunate, '. . . apart from faith in God there is really *nothing* (my italics) to be said for the notion of human equality'. Belief in God in the Judaeo-Christian tradition is undoubtedly a strong support for such a belief, and support can be found in other religions, but there are many atheists and agnostics in our society, and it is important that the search for a common morality to undergird the respect for persons should include the widest possible range of beliefs. Our time has seen efforts of public bodies like the United Nations and private ones like Amnesty International to work in this area. Undoubtedly their work is fragile; all the more reason to support it. (*ii*) There has been the growth of industrial chaplaincies, so that there are far more in industry who have been specifically helped to relate the Christian faith to industry than when Temple wrote. Surprisingly little of the thinking of 'industrial mission' has as yet appeared in print, but it surely will before long. This growth is part of the much greater stress in the church on the role of the laity, exactly as Temple wished, though one would like to see more signs of that laity in evidence in industry. (*iii*) The ecumenical movement has grown enormously. A Temple writing today could draw on the work of the Geneva Conference of 1966 on 'Christians in the Technical and Social Revolutions of our Time'. It was designed to achieve in its time what the Oxford Conference did in 1937. In 1966 there was a wider frame of reference. It was the most truly ecumenical conference on Christian social ethics ever held, and this made the radical stance it took all the more significant, for it showed that when the more 'established' white churches were no longer so predominant, the radical stance which Temple exemplified came to the fore.[16] Perhaps even more significant, since it was in a sense unofficial, was the fact that the official Assembly of the World Council of Churches meeting at Uppsala two years later did not repudiate it but broadly endorsed it. The new radical notes which came to the fore for the first time in general ecumenical Christian social ethics (together with old ones from Oxford and earlier) have become pervasive since then. Also there has been the *aggiornamento* in the Roman Catholic Church initiated by Pope John XXIII, particularly focused in the Second Vatican Council, 1962–5. For the first time such a Council dealt with the themes covered in the Pastoral Constitution *Gaudium et Spes* (The Church in the Modern World), with results remarkably similar to what was to be the line of the Geneva Conference. Since the Council there has been the papal encyclical *Populorum Progressio*, and the Apostolic Letter of Pope Paul VI to Cardinal Roy, President of the Pontifical Commission for Justice and Peace, *Octogesima Adveniens*, on the eightieth anniversary of the encyclical *Rerum Novarum* which is the foundation of the modern Roman Catholic social teaching. (*iv*) We are now much more used to thinking of the church sociologically. Indeed the sociology of religion as an academic study has had a revival, in the sense of returning to a major preoccupation of the founding fathers of sociology like Durkheim and Weber. This means that the social effects of the church as an institution, and of its internal structure, are looked at more explicitly. So the question of the church's involvement – and especially how it should 'interfere' – can be discussed with more realism. (*v*) There has been the development of a 'political theology' with its various aspects, of which the theologies of hope and liberation, or revolutionary theology as it is sometimes called, are the most significant. One side of theologies of liberation is the acceptance of Marxist categories, a point to which I shall return; on the theological side the strongly eschatological emphasis is a further illustration that radical and positive stances towards this world can be drawn from all aspects of Christian doctrine.

I turn now to six points on the political and social front since Temple's death.

1. The toughness of some social problems has already been mentioned. Others include the fact that we have made hardly any dint in the relative deprivation of the lower-paid worker, that a lot of school leavers go into dead-end jobs, and at the moment are not in a job at all; that the numbers on supplementary benefit do not fall; and that there is much evidence of harm to children in deprived families.

2. The conditions of employment in industry have considerably improved both in themselves, and in terms of redundancy and retraining. The Employment Protection Act which came into force this year will improve things further. But little progress has been made (though more in West Germany, Austria, Denmark, Norway, Sweden and Holland) towards what Temple emphasized so strongly, industrial democracy, or the right of the workers not merely to be informed about, but to be consulted and to participate in, deciding about the conditions of their work and the policies of the company they work for. These

issues seem now to be coming to the front; it remains to be seen
what we shall do about them. I cannot help reflecting ruefully
that the first time I ventured into print after graduating was in
a study booklet on these issues, and more than a generation
later I read in *The Economist* of 11 January 1975, an article ad-
vocating precisely the same thing, which pointed out that until
very recently they have been ignored in Britain, and that while
they can be evaded for some time they cannot be put off for
ever. For 'the need for participation was created by society, not
invented by sociologists, right-wing trade unionists, or capital-
ists trying to breathe new life into a supposedly dying system';
it added that society is 'ever more inclined to contest decisions
taken from on high, ever more educated, and frequently competent to do so. This is true of the shop floor, of white-collar
workers, of every level of management.'

3. We have discovered the Third and Fourth Worlds in a way
and on a scale unmatched a generation ago. The Third World
has forced itself on our attention by providing the first instance
of economic power – oil power – against a wealthy West which
has been used to dictating its own terms of trade. The Fourth
World on the other hand has forced itself on our attention by
its very misery. Modern means of mass communication have
brought this before us in a way hitherto unknown. We are the
first generation to hear the cry of the suffering expressed from
every corner of the world, and knowledge brings responsibility.
It has become more obvious how interdependent we are, and
according to our economic and political power so we affect the
lives of others or are affected ourselves by the decisions of
others. This is a reality which governments and electorates
would rather forget, and one which demands greater skill and
wisdom from both.

4. Inflation is an issue which Temple did not have to face. If
it continues at anything like 15% to 25% per annum for any
number of years it will be more disruptive of the social system
than a world war. Much of it is due to international factors, but
much also depends upon the ability with which it is handled
domestically. The crucial issue to be faced is that no government
can combine three things, all of which many people would like:
a stable price level, full employment, and free collective bargaining. They are incompatible. What social policies provide
the best 'mix' is the issue before Western type democracies.

5. The easy way out of this dilemma has been thought to be

the pursuit of greater affluence. This still has a contribution to make. The advocates of no growth have overstated the case. But they have drawn attention to the need for much more caution and care. Moreover what we do with our wealth becomes an ever more pressing question in the 'one-world' of today.

6. If there are some things it is inherently impossible for governments to do, there are others which are politically impossible. They can adopt in a depression Keynesian policies of tax rebates and increased public spending. This is popular, and it has been effective. But in a boom they cannot deflate by increasing taxes and cutting public expenditure because powerful large companies (some multinational) and trade unions are against it. And society is equally opposed to the other policy of cutting the money supply because it is not prepared to accept the level of unemployment that would ensue. If an open society like ours is to survive it will demand more state activity in promoting public bargaining which relates consumption and investment to resources and productivity. Possibly annual synchronized wage negotiations together with some price restrictions will be needed as part of the most suitable political 'mix'. Evidence from Sweden may be helpful here.

This brings me to the British political tradition. We have had a long continuity of political and social institutions because the gradual break up of medieval structures prepared the way for the British to lead in the development of industry, and thus become wealthy. Time and wealth have been on our side. Nor have we had our institutions forcefully disrupted by foreign invasion. As a result we have developed considerable political skills in government and in social and industrial processes. Can we continue to change smoothly?

One element in our tradition, and how far it is cause and how far effect is probably an unanswerable question, is a strong moral element derived from the Christian faith. Elements in it include (*i*) medieval social thought continuing to the seventeenth century and picked up in the nineteenth, which powerfully influenced Temple; (*ii*) radical Dissent and political offshoots from it; (*iii*) the spin-off from the Methodist movement, particularly in its Primitive Methodist form; (*iv*) more recently the urban working class Roman Catholic element in the Labour Party. This moral element has tended to mitigate social conflicts where a more Marxist frame of thought exacerbates them. Reinhold Niebuhr had a very interesting editorial on this in the journal *Christianity and Society* in the summer of 1943.[17] He was discussing, among other things, the significance of England having as Archbishop of Canterbury a man with social views as radical as those of Temple. 'In other words the moral protest against the injustices of our society is derived from and need not express itself against, the Christian Religion. This one fact makes Britain unique in modern social history. For all the radical movements of the Continent have been anti-Christian. In America they are not anti-Christian but they are predominantly secular. It may be that the unbroken character of the Christian ethos in Britain is also the cause of the unbroken socio-political history since 1688.' But he went on to point out the defect of this virtue, that Britain 'may well maintain many forms of capitalistic injustice because of her ability to mitigate them more successfully than other nations'.

The biggest challenge to this whole way of thinking comes from the liberation and revolutionary theology of Latin America. A good survey can be found in *Revolutionary Theology Comes of Age*, by José Miguez Bonino.[18] In the last resort it depends on accepting the broad validity of a Marxian analysis. Whether it is true for Latin America is not our present business. If it is there is no *theological* reason to deny the revolutionary, political and economic conclusions of so many Latin American theologians.[19] I do not think it is true for Britain, though the question cannot be dealt with here. However, a question which ought to be considered is whether Temple in *Christianity and Social Order* should have more explicitly linked his conclusions to socialism. After all in his youth he did. In an article in *The Economic Review* in 1908[20] he says 'The alternative stands before us – socialism or heresy. . . . In other words, Socialism . . . is the economic realization of the Christian Gospel.' It is sometimes said that later in life he moved to the right politically, and it is true that he did not continue to express himself in this way. But it could be held that the radical questions in *Christianity and Social Order* point that way, and it might be asked whether it was anything more than diplomatic caution which prevented him saying so, perhaps akin to the reasons which made him give up his membership of the Labour Party in 1921, after three years in it.

To this four points may be made.

1. The Christian criticism of capitalism, echoing F. D. Maurice, on the grounds that competition is a lie, and that we should

have production for use and not for profit, is much too simple, as Temple clearly sees in this book. It is rather the institutional structures within which competition is carried on and private property dealt with that need scrutiny.

2. The political case for socialism in the old sense of 'the nationalization of all the means of production, distribution and exchange' has been clouded by the evidence from Russia and her satellites of the dangers of monolithic power structures; and the evidence of communist countries like Yugoslavia or China which in their different ways are trying alternative structures is, so far, ambiguous and not sufficient to clear doubts.

3. Keynesian economic policies overthrew the expectation, widely held in the 1930s, that the capitalist system was breaking down, as the Marxian analysis said it would. Our present difficulties do not show that it must break down, though there is always the possibility that it may do so if enough political wisdom is not shown by governments and electorates in dealing with it. If it does, the result will be a much less open society than the one we have experienced and – I would say – enjoy.

4. There has been an utopianism pervasive in the Labour Movement, associated with a belief in evolutionary progress based on the spread of education. This has become less plausible, and its decline has left many in that movement in something of a spiritual vacuum. The utopian belief was an off-shoot of the Christian-Humanist tradition, and it served as a surrogate for a religious faith. If that has faded, and Marxism with its religious overtones does not seem plausible, a certain emptiness is left; for whatever may be the case with right-wing political movements, a cynical realism (which may appear all that is left as an option) does not go well with left-wing ones. Temple stands for a Christian realism as in various places in this book he implicitly addresses himself to the situation I have described.

There remains his concern for equality for the sake of human fellowship. It lies behind the socialist case and in Temple's view it lies near the heart of the Christian gospel. It leads to the asking of radical questions about the social order. This Temple did. His questions remain as relevant as when he asked them, even though the empirical background is in many respects different. In dealing with them the question of how far the state should control production is a valid but subsidiary one. It is part of a range of questions involving, (*a*) the powers needed by the state for particular necessary economic functions and the

checks needed on the abuse of the power; (*b*) the type and
extent of participation in decision making, and (*c*) the role of
intermediate associations in the light of the principle of
subsidiarity.[21]

Among intermediate associations the churches are of great
importance, and this is why Temple's preoccupation in this
book with the church's involvement (allowing for his stress on
the importance of the Christian in his job and as a citizen)
remains important. Her method of doing so needs constant
reflection, and there has been much ecumenical discussion of
this since the Geneva Conference of 1966. I am thinking, for
example, of Paul Ramsey's book *Who Speaks for the Church?*,[22]
and the debates on the actions of the World Council of Churches
in its Programme to Combat Racism since 1970. Further, the
involvement of the church herself through her ownership and
administration of property and investments has come to the
fore. The ethics of investment and the social responsibilities of
the corporate investor are live issues which will not go away.
They have also come to the fore at a time when the churches
have a smaller membership to rely on for regular giving, too
much property to maintain and (probably) too many paid personnel, and this at a time of high inflation. How they react to
this will be a kind of litmus paper test of their social convictions.
For they need to demonstrate by actions as well as by teaching
that they are indeed on the side of the disadvantaged, and not
only in the sense of 'ambulance work' which deals with disas-
ters, but also in furthering structures which prevent them.
These structures need to express man's freedom in fellowship
without romanticizing him, so that his selfishness is both contained and utilized. However, the less there is of selfishness the
better, so that there is the continued need for personal as well
as for social renewal. To promote both is a task of the church.
It follows from her worship of God through Christ her Lord.

7

Anglican and Ecumenical Styles in Social Ethics

The roots of Anglican social ethics go back to traditional moral theology as it developed in the Western church during the Middle Ages. After the Reformation both Anglican and Puritan moral theology continued broadly in this tradition, though differing somewhat from that of the Roman Catholic Church of the Counter-Reformation, in particular by not being predominantly orientated towards the training of priests, especially as confessors in seminaries. It died out, for reasons that have never been thoroughly clarified, at the end of the seventeenth century.

In consequence, when the vast social changes produced by the Industrial Revolution hit England, a tradition of thinking in social ethics which could deal with social structures had been lost. In the nineteenth century a number of evangelicals identified particular abuses, such as slavery and the slave trade, or the use of boy chimney sweeps, and campaigned to remove them by legislative action, but they had no social theology as such. It was F. D. Maurice who worked out a social theology and although of course, like any thinker, others influenced him (notably Coleridge), he had very little to go on in this area and his contribution was truly creative. He himself soon moved more into pioneering work in adult education, but he left a legacy of theological thought in social ethics which sparked off quite a lot of diverse social theology and which lasted until well into this century. It was partly the inspiration of the COPEC Conference at Birmingham in 1924. After this its influence was fed into the wider setting of ecumenical social ethics which was launched at the Stockholm Conference in 1925 or, in Anglican terms, primarily into the Christendom group, which did claim to pursue a distinctive Anglican (Catholic) path until it largely folded up after the Second World War.

Development in moral theology

Meanwhile Kenneth Kirk's attempt to bring moral theology back into the service of the Anglican Church by adapting to its use the main tradition of Roman Catholic moral theology was more directed towards internal problems of church life and practice than to social ethics (though he did not ignore it). In his notable *Conscience and Its Problems*[1] the issues which occur in the area of social ethics are discussed under the headings of 'Doubt' and 'Perplexity'. His broad conclusions, however, are very free and flexible (pp. 375f.) though not very fully worked out. They present no barriers to assumptions and methods which have subsequently been developed by Anglicans and in the ecumenical movement for getting to grips with the economic, social, industrial and political issues of our rapidly changing twentieth-century society. One reason for this is that by the time Kirk returned to traditional moral theology its two traditional courts of appeal for authority, the Bible and Natural Law, could no longer be used in the way they had been in the past. The development of critical studies of the Bible and in philosophy had undermined the traditional use of both. Hence the flexibility to which Kirk was led. It is the coming to terms with this which has produced the vast changes in Roman Catholic moral theology in the last twenty years. The problem had been postponed for it by the practical embargo on critical biblical studies in that church following upon the Modernist controversy and by the emphasis on papal authority after the Infallibility Decree of the First Vatican Council. The pluralism in Roman Catholic thought which has followed the Second Vatican Council has had as great an effect in moral theology as anywhere. Yet in this as in every other area of theology in the church matters are not resolved neatly. Old and new interpretations remain. In particular there is pre-occupation with the authority of a *magisterium*, which can speak within one framework in *Populorum Progressio* and another in *Humanae Vitae* in successive years. But there is no doubt of the general tendency among the moral theologians. This has brought them in their methods and preoccupations very much alongside Anglican and ecumenical social ethics; and the creation in 1968 of SODEPAX, the joint agency of the World Council of Churches and the Pontifical Commission 'Justitia et Pax', with its concern for society, development and peace, indicated no more than the beginnings of a structural relationship which reflects a common outlook and way of working which would have been unthinkable before Vatican II.

The contribution of J. H. Oldham

I suppose no one did more to establish this way of working than that notable Anglican layman and ecumenical pioneer, Dr J. H. Oldham. The theology behind it is contained in his section of the book *The Church and its Function in Society*, which he wrote jointly with Dr W. A. Visser't Hooft, and which was given beforehand to all the delegates to the Oxford Conference on 'Church, Community and State' in 1937. At this time it was said that the churches would do well if they arrived in a quarter of a century where that book already was, but in the event the Second World War speeded things up, and it was broadly pre-supposed when the WCC was able officially to get started at Amsterdam in 1948.

Oldham's method was to get together groups of people with varied and relevant experience in the area of social ethics under discussion, to establish the key facts and the main trends in the situation, examine possible ways of action, and evaluate them by criteria deriving from the Christian faith (though they might not be exclusive to it), in the hopes of getting agreement as to the general direction in which change should be worked for, without expecting detailed agreement at the level of specific policies. (This middle level he called 'middle axioms'.) The method can be applied to small or large issues, within a small or large area, with one confessional tradition or among many, with Christians only or enlisting others if they have relevant and necessary experience and expertise. Variations of it underlie nearly all substantial work done by the churches in social ethics. The corollary is that one cannot get to particular and detailed conclusions direct from any specifically Christian source, Bible, church, or Natural Law (as interpreted by the church). There will always be a final step involving empirical data and an estimate of its relative significance, as well as an estimate of the likely consequences of possible lines of action, about which conscientious Christian opinion may well differ. Church strategies must allow for this.

This is not universally agreed. There are those who want to avoid the ambiguity of Christian social ethics by taking a direct step from some Christian source to a specific conclusion. Some do it from Christian doctrine. In a sense this is what F. D. Maurice did in his attack on competition in favour of what he called socialism (its practical outcome was the series of producers' co-operatives). Traditional moral theology and the Christendom group thought one could do this on the basis of Natural Law. In World Council of Churches' circles many under the influences of biblical theology, which itself was much influenced by Karl Barth and in this respect echoes the Calvinist tradition, have thought one could do it by moving directly from a biblical text or passage to a detailed specific conclusion on a current ethical question. Now biblical theology has collapsed, but liberation theologians have continued something of the same tendency in their use of the Exodus saga. The ecumenical movement in social ethics has often made progress when a broad consensus on what should be done has been achieved by those who nevertheless approached it on the basis of different theological methods.

The reciprocity of insight and expertise

A second issue arises in what I have called the Oldham method. It presupposes a reciprocal relation between insights derived from the Christian faith and an analysis of the empirical situation. This means that it is necessary to take factual data seriously, but it is also to let theological insight provide a critique of the value judgments explicit or implicit in the experience or expertise called upon. Facts are vital, but often any fact worth using is seen in a context of significance which makes it stand out amid the manifold data of human life, and this involves value judgments. This is the case even in the natural sciences but much more so in the social sciences. All evidence needs examining from the point of view from which it is presented. Christians have often made the mistake of ignoring evidence, but they can also be uncritical in the face of expert evidence. The Christendom group made many foolish mistakes in the realm of economics through its mistaken *a priori* use of Natural Law, but it raised very urgent questions about the presuppositions of much allegedly neutral expertise. Today the liberation theologians of Latin America, who see that the Christian faith cannot by itself establish particular political and social policies, go on to say that a 'science' of society is needed and then assume, almost without question, that a version of Marxism will supply this. This is a major assumption which has to be argued for and cannot be established (as they see) on purely Christian grounds. But it will not do to take Marxism's claims to be 'scientific' on its own terms. There is no escape from getting to grips with the claim, and in doing so part of the task will be to bring Christian categories to bear on what in Marxism is presented in the form of a scientific theory.

To return to the Oxford Conference. Notable theological contributions are enshrined in the six volumes of essays written for it and published afterwards, much of them still relevant and of a quality which has not since been surpassed. Anglicans made contributions with others; confessional differences seemed secondary when faced with the twin evils of totalitarianism and mass unemployment which dominated the scene. 'Doctrine divides but service unites' had been the slogan of Stockholm. This has often been the case, but not always. We have recently seen in the case of reactions to racism that the reverse can happen. But in neither case does it follow that divisions fall along confessional lines. Indeed they seem more often to cross them. For instance the more pietist and individualist type of evangelical theology is found as an anti-ecumenical minority position in several confessional traditions. This is one reason why we must be cautious about claims for a distinctively Anglican social ethic.

It was the World Council of Churches' Geneva Conference of 1966 which launched a whole series of issues which have been the preoccupation of Christian social ethics ever since. It followed the 'Oldham' method of getting informed group preparatory work done and mutually checked and cross-checked, on a world scale. Geneva was not a turning point in its method but it was in its range. It was immediately preceded by Vatican II, whose Pastoral Constitution *Gaudium et Spes* (The Church in the Modern World) represented in many ways a change of method as well, so that, as I have said, ever since then the Roman Catholic Church and the World Council of Churches have been very similar in their general position in social ethics (certain population questions apart). Geneva was the most truly ecumenical consultation in its field ever held. In addition to its ecumenical range, with the Orthodox well represented and a number of active Roman Catholic participant observers, it made a notable attempt to bring in representatives of churches from the Third World in such proportionate numbers that it could no longer be a Western occasion in terms of priorities and procedures in which others are incorporated but do not shape. It proved a radical consultation, concerned with technological, political and cultural revolution to an extent which was a shock to those who came from churches with a 'Christendom' background, who had been in the habit of backing the *status quo*, and who had not realized the speed of change. It marked the end of Eurocentrism and of a conservative form of a theology of the orders of creation. In this context of the search for a responsible world society questions of economic development, racialism, the violence of established order as against that of a just revolution, and technological and especially nuclear invention have been a continued preoccupation, merging into the theme of a just, participatory and sustainable society.

Western Christians under attack

It has been an uncomfortable time for Churches in Western countries. The agenda has been much the same the world over (except that environmental issues seem to the Third/Fourth World a luxury it cannot afford), but it has been seen very differently by the wealthy and by the rest. In particular the whites, who are predominantly wealthy and in 'Christian' countries have been living through a time when they can do nothing right, so strong has been the reaction against their former political but now more economic hegemony. It was said half humorously that to be white, male, ordained and middle-aged was almost to be written off at the WCC Nairobi Assembly. Moreover churches in the West have been slow to allow their traditional preoccupations to be called in question by the very different urgencies of the churches in the Third/Fourth world. It is difficult to gainsay that in the words of the January 1978 editorial in *Church Alert* (The SODEPAX journal) one also sees 'a general indifference and apathy when looking at the ghetto mentalities of western societies'. The World Council of Churches (and the Vatican) is much more open to pressures which come from the non-Western parts of the world, and this has produced some tensions between the World Council of Churches and the Western churches.

The Church of England has shared this tension. Yet it has

been influenced by ecumenical developments. A case in point is the aftermath of the grants given since 1970 by the World Council of Churches in its Programme to Combat Racism to (among many others) some resistance movements who were in armed revolt against their *de facto* governments. The General Synod of the Church of England was led to set up a special Commission on *Civil Strife* which produced a perceptive report in 1971. It would not have done this without the jolt produced by the action of the World Council of Churches, and its tone and content would have been very different prior to the Geneva Conference of 1966.

The Anglican Communion is now showing the same stresses and range of reaction in these matters as the World Council of Churches' wider constituency. In this connection a study of the 'Church and Society' sections of the three reports from the Anglican Consultative Council, set up after the Lambeth Conference of 1968, is interesting.

1. *Limuru, Kenya, 1971*

Out of 54 members 26 were from the 'Third' world, thus repeating the Geneva 1966 pattern and, as at Geneva, it is clear that the West did not dominate the proceedings. On race the report remarks that actions speak louder than words and then commends –

> The action of the Episcopal Church in the USA in giving grants to the poor and dispossessed in areas of community development and social change.
> The World Council of Churches' grants. It does this on the grounds that 'the Church has an obligation to empower the powerless in situations of violence where power is being destructively imposed'. With reference to the World Council of Churches' grants, it says 'In our judgment no public action of the Churches during the past 25 years has done so much to arouse public discussion on a moral issue. It has given to ordinary people an indication of the fact that the Churches are ready to stand by the oppressed and exploited even when there is some risk to themselves.

On the question of power, and violent and non-violent social and political change the Council recommended close attention to the work of the World Council of Churches and the fullest possible Anglican participation in it. It regretted that so little was done on the matter by the provinces of the Anglican Communion. It commended a statement of the Central Committee of the World Council of Churches at Addis Ababa in 1971 concerned with non-violent methods of achieving social change but which referred to the 'growing unwillingness to condemn categorically those groups, including Christians, who resort to violence in the face of massive, entrenched social, racial and economic injustice'.

2. *Dublin, 1973*

The Council's report deals with most of these issues under the theme of 'Education: a Process of Liberation for Social Justice'; it begins boldly, 'It is necessary to understand that the injustice that exists in pluralist societies is violent by nature', and goes on to develop a biblically based theology of liberation before reaching education. This, it says, can either domesticate or liberate, and it argues against formal and élitist education in favour of non-formal educational programmes. For the rest, Christians and church leaders are encouraged to make courageous commitments to social justice and to give financial support to oppressed groups. The oppressed must take the lead in dialogue with the oppressor. And Christians who hold diverse opinions in these matters are to maintain a dialogue within the one Christian fellowship in site of the tensions between them.

3. *Trinidad, 1976*

This strikes a new note before dealing with the familiar specific issues. It refers to F. D. Maurice and William Temple and affirms that 'there is now intense theological discussion in progress on social questions throughout the Christian Churches, but the Anglican contribution to this has hardly been significant . . .'. Nevertheless the Anglican Communion may yet have a distinctive contribution to make not so much in specific types of social action but as 'an authentic pattern of corporate life and relationships'. With due penitence for failures we may see it as a 'prototype community', an 'alternative society', an inspiration, a pattern, 'a first fruit of the reconciled community which God will one day bring into being for the whole world'. This is particularly in respect of three characteristics. (*i*) a community of unity in diversity; (*ii*) its practice of mutual service between equals; (*iii*) its structure and order which fosters the growth of individual responsibility, and also the subordination to one another within an hierarchical structure, by searching for an authentically pastoral style of leadership.

This, however, still leaves us to make theological and moral judgments, and at times 'prophetic utterances and clear social stances'. So it goes on to discuss violence, more cautiously than the two previous meetings. It records the growing opinion that armed revolt may be the lesser of two evils, but says that this is so only in utterly exceptionable cases, and that the church should seek new effective forms of positive non-violent action. In a section on human rights it warns against utopianism, and says that 'Christians on the spot must decide what their witness should be however much they are challenged or supported by their membership of a world-wide Christian community'.

A prototype social order?

The claim that the nature of the Anglican Communion provides the prototype of a proper social order is one that requires careful thought. It could easily be dismissed with ridicule. Yet there must be something in it to an Anglican. If he did not think Anglicanism witnesses to the best available form of church life he would presumably leave it for another. Today this is fully compatible with a deep ecumenical commitment. The Orthodox must presumably have the same thoughts when they talk of *sobornost*. But the greater the claims one makes for a particular theory of church life and order, the bigger the gulf between theory and practice will be seen to be. Reinhold Niebuhr once said when asked why he remained in the Evangelical and Reformed Church in the USA that one can only tolerate the follies of the church one is born in. Take the claim about Anglicanism as a community of unity and diversity. It can in fact exhibit incoherence leading to paralysis. The Church of England's rejection of unity with Methodism is an instance.

However, there is the further question, assumed at Trinidad, that a model of church life can be transferred to society at large, and in most cases a plural society at that. Is this not to collapse two kingdoms into one? If, for instance management structures in industry are to exhibit a peculiarly Anglican principle of 'subordination to one another within an hierarchical structure', or politicians are to give an 'authentically pastoral style of leadership' like the one for which Anglicans are searching, it needs much more spelling out if it is to be taken seriously. On the other hand there is a good case for saying that there are a number of procedures of natural justice which apply to the structures of the world, which the church herself on occasion may need reminding to observe. I agree with Brian Barry in his book *The Liberal Theory of Justice*,[2] which is a discussion of John Rawl's *A Theory of Justice*,[3] that there are three broad models of society, the hierarchical, the individualist liberal and the altruistic collaborative. A viable social order will need to embody elements of all three. Crucial questions arise over the particular 'mix'. It is to these that Christian social ethics must address itself.

What has the Church of England been up to recently in this area? If one takes the General Synod as the voice of the church it is overwhelmingly middle- and upper middle-class in composition. In economic matters it usually agrees with the usual opinions of its class, but not always. Recently, although its members have little or no personal experience of trade unions or contact with them, it has resisted any temptation to 'union bashing', and on the question of the closed shop it has received from its Board of Social Responsibility a document very uncharacteristic of the attitudes of the class it represents. On some other questions, capital punishment and questions of immigration to mention two, it has shown itself much more radical than the public at large, including its own general church constituency.

The Board of Social Responsibility is partly occupied with the 'establishment' concern of feeding the bishops in the House of Lords with material for their speeches, with the result that their interventions have become noticeably better informed. The church also feels on occasions a responsibility for suggesting improvements in the law of the land, which of course applies to all, independently of what the church's opinion on what the 'law' for committed church members should be. It did this on divorce. It hopes to influence decision makers by a steady stream of reports on social issues, always the result of group work which is technically well informed, though perhaps inclined to be somewhat élitist in its range of contacts.

However, in these latter activities (that is to say those not connected with the House of Lords), the Church of England works no differently from other churches, like the Methodist, or from the way churches work together in reports and documents provided by the British Council of Churches, or in the evidence produced on behalf of that body on the development of nuclear energy to the recent Windscale enquiry on reprocessing spent nuclear fuel.

Questions to the British churches

Broadly speaking the British churches are at home in their society. They are conscious of its Jewish-Christian-classical humanist background. They know it is far from perfect, but they do not see it as fundamentally wrong at any major point. Even the most radical Christians want to challenge society to follow policies which they think implement more fully Christian and human values to which it is already committed. The churches are also conscious of a still latent though much reduced power to sway public opinion. There is nothing like the head-on collision over a basic policy like *apartheid*, or kindred manifestations of it, nor a sense of the hopeless corruption and injustice of one's own government which is the judgment of many Latin American Christians. Since we must deal with our own situation and not someone else's there is in one sense nothing to cavil at in this. But a question must be raised as to whether relatively wealthy British churches are sufficiently conscious of how they appear to their fellow Christians in the two thirds of the world which by comparison is extremely poor. And another question is how far they have faced up to the extent to which the institutional financial interests of the church, especially as it copes with inflation, serve to blinker moral judgments. Distrust of prophetic gestures can cover a reluctance to side with the poor and oppressed. Moreover it does not seem to occur to the Church of England that it might be helped in seeing its own social role more clearly by asking Anglicans from elsewhere, let alone those of other confessions, to join with it in investigating them. Driven by the impasse of the Irish situation, the Church of Ireland has recently done precisely this in an effort to come to grips with the grievous situation it has to live with. In the rest of the British Isles, the churches are not conscious of any issue desperate enough to drive them to seek such help. The wealthy are often blind to their true state.

I have just referred to prophetic gestures. There are two broad tendencies in Christian ethics which the church has faced ever since St Paul wrestled with the recalcitrant Corinthian Christians. Borrowing terms from Max Weber's famous essay on 'Politics as a Vocation' they can be called an ethic of ultimate ends and an ethic of responsibility. (Compare II Cor. 6.14ff. for the former and I Cor. 5.9ff. for the latter.) Both are represented in the World Council of Churches and in the Anglican Communion. Both have their advantages and disadvantages. An ethic of ultimate ends is 'prophetic'. It strikes a broad attitude. It condemns what is wrong. It speaks of an eschatological hope often in apocalyptic terms. It does not deal with details of policies and remedies. An ethic of responsibility is concerned with detailed analysis, with the 'nicely calculated less or more', with adjustments to the wider plural society. Prophecy can be irresponsible. An ethic of responsibility can become timid and over-cautious; it too needs to live in an eschatological dimension. Prophecy can exaggerate the power of the church and confuse words and gestures with real gains. It is salutary to reflect that the sociologist of religion casts it in a predominantly conserving role, along with law, and makes no exception for Christianity. And yet the prophetic element in the Judaeo-Christian tradition cannot be gainsaid, and it is something with which the sociologist of religion does not find it easy to deal.

No specifically Anglican social ethic

I have been writing of 'ideal types', exaggerating the contrasts between the two. They are not necessarily totally opposed nor each incapable of influencing the other. But to return to where I began, this distinction is not distinctively Anglican. This is not surprising. Anglicans do not usually claim any peculiarly Anglican doctrine, but to have embodied a way of holding fundamentals together (witness talk of the Lambeth Quadrilateral). So we can hardly expect or want a distinctive social ethic.

Nor is there a distinctively Anglican way of relating to a plural society. As already mentioned only the Christendom group in recent times thought there was, when it talked of a Catholic Christian Sociology. The group has now been fruitfully reconstituted with a rather different emphasis. Developments in moral theology passed it by, as the liturgical changes which followed Vatican II have passed by the kind of Anglo-Catholicism it represented. In perspective it was as much irrelevant to the main issues in social ethics as were the struggles between Anglicans and Nonconformists in the nineteenth century over Establishment.

It seems clear that no one confessional tradition can any longer handle the world's social issues alone, if it ever could Not even Rome. Certainly Anglicans, who represent one in forty of the world's Christians cannot, not even in England, a country where it represents the dominant tradition. We are better employed in doing together with other Christians everything that conscience does not compel us to do separately. There will be little of the latter in social ethics. If some distinctive Anglican contribution emerges, let it. But this will not happen by trying to cultivate it directly and demarcating it in advance.

8

From Oxford to Nairobi

It was thirty years ago that the World Council of Churches was formally constituted and held its first Assembly at Amsterdam. Nothing like it has been seen before in the history of the church. It is an expression of the ecumenical movement which, although its origins can be found just before the First World War, was primarily provoked into life by the appalling catastrophe of that war. The churches were implicated in it. Their divisions and their isolation from each other had impeded their witness. A movement for renewal and unity – and it is important to note that renewal was as much a concern as unity – gathered momentum. Part of it was concerned with centuries-old doctrinal and ecclesiological divisions, or faith and order, and with that I am not on this occasion concerned. Part was concerned with renewal for the service of men in the cause of peace and social justice, what became known as 'life and work'.

It is difficult to exaggerate how isolated the churches were from one another in 1914 and how uninformed and ineffective was their social witness. With their roots in a predominantly rural world whose pace of social change was very slow, if not imperceptible, they had proved quite unable to cope with the dramatic urbanization and speed of social change brought about by the Industrial Revolution.

The pioneers in the ecumenical movement were very conscious of this. On the life and work side the first major event was a conference of church leaders at Stockholm in 1925. However for our purposes it is the second major conference of the movement at Oxford in 1937 which is of most significance. Its theme was 'Church, Community and State'. It met against the background of brutal Nazi and Fascist totalitarian governments on the one hand, and the aftermath of the economic crash of 1929 with its mass unemployment on the other.

The Oxford Conference was carefully prepared beforehand. Leading theologians and other experts from different countries contributed papers which were circulated, commented on and then rewritten, and in the end produced work of a quality which has not since been equalled and much of which is still valuable. The Oxford Conference marked a recovery of a doctrine of the church. 'Let the church be the church' was the phrase in which this was summed up. Much Protestantism in the nineteenth and early twentieth centuries had been individualistic, suspicious of the church, doubtful of whether Jesus ever thought of one, and prone to stress instead the kingdom of God which it saw as an ideal social order, a kind of co-operative commonwealth which men were to build on earth.

The picture presented by the Roman Catholic Church in the nineteenth century, especially after the Vatican Council of 1870, only confirmed it in this view. However, biblical scholarship undermined it, and totalitarian political pressures brought home the centrality of the church to Christian faith and witness, even as it made the churches healthily self-critical of their own failures. The Oxford Conference faced these realistically even as it indicated ways in which churches as corporate bodies and individual Christians should relate to economic, social and political affairs. In particular it stressed the role of the layman in his job, and as a citizen, as the main instrument of Christian social influence. This has subsequently borne much fruit.

The second war followed shortly afterwards, but it was the Oxford Conference which enabled leaders of the ecumenical movement to keep in touch with one another during the Second World War. There was none of the egregious jingoism which marked the churches in the First World War. In many ways from an ecumenical point of view it was an international civil war. So much so that it proved comparatively easy to pick up the threads of the ecumenical movement when it was over, and to bring the World Council of Churches into being in 1948, formed from 147 churches in 44 countries. That, however, was the time of the cold war. The United States of America was by far the wealthiest nation with by far the strongest churches and was therefore paying the greater part of the costs of the Council. If the American churches had tried to get numerical representation in proportion to their numbers or exercise influence in proportion to their wealth it would have been disastrous. But they have had the wisdom and forbearance to see this and have never tried to do so. Nevertheless in the thick of the cold war, and with few Christians present from Communist lands, it would have been easy for the churches implicitly or explicitly to back uncritically the social and political ideas of the Western allies. But they did not. Careful theological thought led to the concept of 'the responsible society' as a suitable criterion, derived from the Christian faith, by which to evaluate social and political policies. It was to play a considerable part in ecumenical social ethics for the next twenty years. It led to critical questions being addressed both to the centralized socialist economies of the Russian type, and to the social market economies of the West with their various stages of welfare capitalism. It meant the forswearing of any uncritical social conformism on the part of the churches (which had been their standard practice for centuries). At the same time the Amsterdam Assembly stressed strongly the role of the church as servant, the opposite of the triumphalist attitude it had taken for so long.

Up to then the ecumenical movement had been predominantly Western in its composition. That is to say it had been drawn overwhelmingly from Europe as the heart of the old Christendom, and from those countries in other continents which were offshoots of that civilization. Its opponents also accused it of being pan-Protestant. But things were soon to alter in both respects. The accession of the large Russian Orthodox Church in 1961 after many years of negotiation (bringing other Orthodox Churches from Eastern Europe in its train) vastly strengthened the Orthodox influence. It was for most of the Orthodox churches a new experience, because for most of their history they have lived under hostile Turkish or atheist governments, although their tradition had been that of Byzantium. Also as a result of the Second Vatican Council of 1962–5 there have been much closer relations with the Roman Catholic Church.

Again in 1961 the International Missionary Council, which had been the meeting place of the younger churches, merged with the World Council and brought with it a stream of churches from Asia, Africa and Latin America with new inter-cultural problems and viewpoints. The preoccupations and hardened ecclesiastical lines of Europe meant little to them.

The World Council discovered what we generally call the

'Third World' just as the era of political de-colonialization was
in full swing. It began a study of rapid social change in Asia,
Africa and Latin America, bringing out both similarities and
differences in the three, and for the first time enabling churches
in the rest of the world to get an up-to-date overall analysis of
what was going on. It soon became clear that rapid social change
was not confined to the Third World. Indeed it was also characteristic of the churches' heartland – Europe, North America
and Australasia. So the idea was conceived of a Conference in
Geneva dealing with 'Christians in the Technical and Social
Revolutions of our Time'. The hope was that, with the same
careful preparation, this conference would do for the ecumenical movement in the mid-sixties what the Oxford Conference
had done 29 years previously. It met in 1966 and was probably
the most truly ecumenical conference ever held. Roman Catholics who had played a significant part in the preparation of the
Pastoral Constitution on 'The Church and the Modern World'
of Vatican II were active as participant observers. The Orthodox
were present in significant numbers.[1] Strenuous efforts were
made to ensure strong representation of the churches from the
Third World to such an extent that they would exert real influence and not be part of a process arranged by the churches of
the First World. Black and brown skins were seen everywhere
(and some yellow). Moreover, the clerics did not dominate;
there were large numbers of Christian laymen with a great deal
of expertise in their own field. The result was a very radical
conference, at least for those who came from Europe and especially North America.

It was in Geneva in 1966 that representatives of the European
and North American churches realized that their views no
longer automatically carry the day, that they no longer set the
agenda and that things look very different, and priorities are
very different in the Third World.

The themes and the implications of Geneva 1966 have been
with us ever since. It was there that Latin American liberation
theology first struck home, and it was there that a Christian talk
of revolution was first seriously heard. Revolutions are of course
of various kinds, and this was subsequently to be spelled out.
At bottom they refer to very rapid and drastic change, such as
we are finding characteristic of the development of biology or
technology. But revolution can also refer to political change, not

necessarily by force but also not excluding it. And it has been new to find Christian social ethics having to take this seriously.

Geneva was a study conference, not speaking *for* the churches but *to* them, and it was a real question whether when the official representatives of the churches met two years later in the World Council Assembly at Uppsala, they would repudiate the drastic thoughts of Geneva. But they did not. And from then to the next and most recent Assembly at Nairobi in 1975, and indeed still, the Geneva themes are being further worked on and refined in both study and practical action.

The concern has been summed up in the phrase 'the search for a just, participatory and sustainable society', the theme of another Geneva type Conference due to be held at Massachusetts Institute of Technology in the summer of 1979.[2]

The wider the range of reference, the harder these themes are to co-ordinate or hold together. In particular the reaction against the white colonial and post-colonial dominance in the Third World is so great that at present whites can do nothing right.

As part of their search for a society which is just and sustainable, thoughtful Christians in the First World have become preoccupied with questions about the limits to growth (especially population), and ecological and environmental problems, some of them connected with the hazards of the development of nuclear energy. Unfortunately all of these hesitations tend to be regarded by the Third World as devices whereby the wealthy First World holds on to what it has got and excludes them from sharing in it. But I do not think these issues can be dismissed so easily.

The wealthy and powerful are for the most part white, and therefore questions of colour inevitably come into the discussion. Which brings me to the one action of the WCC which has produced more reaction than any of its studies. This was the establishment in 1970 of the Programme to Combat Racism (and especially white racialism, because it is the most powerful). The programme has given grants to various anti-racialist organizations for educational and welfare purposes. In the first allocation, four out of seventeen of the organizations were engaged in guerrilla warfare in Africa against their *de facto* Portuguese governments. (Subsequently of course, the movements have taken over as the governments in Angola, Mozambique and Guinea-Bissau.)

The first reaction to the grants in some churches of the First World, especially Britain and West Germany, was outcry. Nevertheless the grants have done a great deal to focus thought. There has been further controversy in the last three weeks about grants to the humanization work of movements fighting against the present Rhodesian government. But again it will come to be realized that, unless one argues from a pacifist position, it is difficult to fault the WCC. After all none of the main church confessional traditions has ever held a totally pacifist position or maintained that an existing government is always to be obeyed.

The WCC has been no more successful than the churches in previous centuries in resolving the difference between pacifist and non-pacifist Christians. Pacifists remain a small, dedicated and creative minority in most Christian churches. Fruitful studies of violence, non-violence and the struggle for social justice have been made by the WCC and they have illuminated the problem, drawn on the experience of those living in situations of great tension and conflict, and asked serious questions of both pacifists and non-pacifists, but they have not resolved the difference between them.

The Stockholm Conference of 1925 had thought that doctrine divides but service unites. Events have proved this isn't always so: service can divide those who are agreed in doctrine, as the Programme to Combat Racism does. But doctrine can also provide shocks. The so-called black theology, which has come mostly from the USA rather than Africa, is a shock to the white Christians on first reading. My experience is that it makes even the most liberal student really angry at first. It is a further sign of the shock that comes when white assumptions are repudiated, and of the enormously different strains which are now explicit within the Christian churches and which find expression in the World Council.

Can the council survive the strain? In one sense its problems are no greater than those of the Vatican. Ever since Vatican II it has been evident that the same stresses are found within the global frame of reference of the Roman Catholic Church. But the Vatican presides over a much more centralized and hierarchical system than does the WCC. The council's task of holding together by now some 286 churches in 90 countries amidst all the diverse strains of the churches in the world today may therefore be the harder.

Yet its bonds may be firmer than appears. There have been, and still are, tensions between what are sometimes called the horizontal and the vertical approaches to the Christian faith and life. The horizontalists see salvation in social as well as personal terms; they seek for 'a society with a human face', embodying creativity, participation, justice and peace for all, and solidarity with the poor and oppressed on the way to it; they preach the need for a *pro*-worldly asceticism as distinct from an *other*-worldly or *inner*-worldly one; they see that the unity of the church is related to the unity of mankind in what is now commonly called a 'village world', and that this involves a new and more subtle meeting of Christians with adherents of other faiths. The verticalists stress more strongly the need for evangelism in the old sense, underlining the uniqueness of Christianity. They are suspicious of political entanglements, and fear the dangers of syncretism. It was thought that there would be a series of dramatic clashes between adherents of these two attitudes at the Nairobi Assembly which would make the news headlines. In fact there was not. 'Confessing Christ today' was the subject most assembly participants wanted to discuss, and a strong conviction took hold of the assembly that Christians must hold fast by one another, despite political, economic and social tensions between them. They must be reconcilers in the midst of conflicts even if they cannot avoid them.

That is good news, and good news does not make headlines. It became clear that to a large extent neither wanted to affirm what the other denied. Moreover the Roman Catholic Synod of Bishops and an Evangelical Congress on World Evangelism at Lausanne, which both met in 1974, were saying much the same thing. There really is a broad consensus emerging among thoughtful Christian people, which is light years away from the dismal situation in 1914.

However the WCC survives only by excellence. It is no use to the churches if it only echoes them, or acts merely as a post-box between them. It needs to be ahead of them, spurring them on, though not too far ahead, or it will be ignored. Those who think it is too far ahead almost invariably come from relatively affluent white churches. Its work can only carry the authority of its own cogency. In this connection its record of far-seeing study in the realm of church and society, the area I have been concerned with in this talk, has been first rate. It has brought experts in, and won their confidence, experts with whom church bodies rarely have contact. It has been far-seeing in bringing issues like nuclear energy before the churches. It has been one of the main agencies through which the churches have been brought really up to date with what is happening in society, for the first time since the break-up of medieval civilization. At least they now have the chance of acting relevantly.

Will the WCC survive another thirty years? It doesn't want to! Its aim is to liquidate itself, to be the catalyst which brings unity to the churches together with renewal. But church structures are tough. Maybe it will take more than another thirty years to change them, though I hope not. In any event the legacy of the method of work in social ethics will be needed. For the moment we need to pay more attention to what the WCC is saying and doing. It has a fine record of giving a hearing in its consultations to individuals and groups involved in the most intense situations of conflict and oppression. They are divided between themselves, and nearly all of what they say is likely to be distasteful to Western Christians, at least on first hearing. Sometimes no clear line emerges, but we all end up much more aware of the way things look to our fellow Christians and of the often agonizing choices they have to make.

But it is not only distaste which hampers serious attention to the WCC. There is also insularity. In the English-speaking world Britain has proved the most insular country as far as the WCC is concerned, the one where it is least well reported and the churches pay least attention to it. This has been typical of the British churches in other ways, for instance their lack of interest in Christians in the other countries of the European Economic Community.

We too easily assume in Britain that our present church structures, priorities and ways of thinking are normal, in the sense that they accurately represent theological differences and accurately reflect the world today. Deviations from them are to be judged by what *we* consider normal. The challenge of the WCC is precisely to our canons of normality.

9

The Right to Work

Theological foreword

This paper is being written for the Commission of a Christian Consultation and I assume that the theological framework within which it operates is made clear in the total context of the proceedings, and that there is therefore no need to elaborate it here. I content myself with the mention of three points which underlie my own approach.

1. The general discussion of human rights is often difficult for the Christian to latch on to because it appears to be cast in individualist terms, whereas for the Christian it is always the person-in-community which is central. The New Testament stresses the new community in which each Christian helps the other to achieve together our full activity in Christ. The problem of how this approach (which the church with all her advantages is far from realizing in practice) can bear upon the civil communities in which human beings perforce live is the old and ongoing Augustinian one of living in Two Cities at one and the same time.

2. Christian theologies vary when approaching human rights between an emphasis on creation and one on christology, but none of the great themes of Christian theology – creation, covenant, incarnation, eschatology – can be neglected, and they must arrive at a theological approach which comes to terms with growingly plural societies, and the necessity of Christians working with those of other faiths and ideologies in the sphere of human rights.

3. There are always conflicts in the field of human rights, e.g., between the individual and the collective, over rights and

duties and over gulfs between overall declarations and actual legal enforcement. Rights are always ambiguous; they do not consist of a fixed content which can be appropriated without any reference to the context, or to other rights. There will always be scope for a critique of empirical manifestations of human institutions with respect to human rights.

Examples of the right to work in recent constitutions, declarations and conventions

USSR 1936, Article 118 guarantees employment and payment according to quality and quantity of work. (This has influenced other Marxist-Socialist states).

India 1949, Article 41. The State within the limits of its economic capacity and development shall make effective provision for the right to work . . .

China, 1954, Article 91. Citizens of the Peoples' Republic of China have the right to work.

Venezuela 1961, Article 61. Work is a duty and a right.

Egypt 1964, Article 216. Work in the United Arab Republic is a right, a duty and an honour for every able citizen.

Universal Declaration of Human Rights, 1948, Article 23. Everyone has the right to work, to free choice of employment (and to rest and leisure).

International Convention on Economic, Social and Cultural Rights, 1961, Article 6 recognizes the right to work freely chosen and accepted.

International Convention on the elimination of all forms of Racial Discrimination, 1960, Article 5, asserts the right to work and to free choice of employment.

This is echoed in various other documents, e.g., of the International Labour Organization, Discrimination (Employment and Occupation) Convention 1958 (repeated in the ILO Employment Policy Convention 1960) and the European Social Charter, 1961.

This is to move from political to economic and social human rights

1. However in an important sense they remain in the political sphere because human rights cannot be a-political. Economic and social ones cannot be divorced from a political framework.

2. The Universal Declaration of Human Rights and the European Convention on Human Rights aim to safeguard human freedom and autonomy against arbitrary state action and allow for the right to dissent and be a nonconformist. This is a freedom of autonomy as against a freedom of participation. (In fact a freedom of autonomy cannot be absolute. How far is there a right to 'drop out'? Many of those who recently were stressing the right to 'do your own thing' presupposed a level of social security support below which they could not fall.)

3. Emphasizing political rights requires the state to do less; emphasizing economic rights requires it to do more.

4. There is a tendency in ecumenical documents on human rights to an exaggeration which obscures their ambiguities:

(*a*) The St Pölten (Austria) Consultation of the Churches' Commission on International Affairs 1974 on Human Rights and Christian Responsibility, Report of Working Group A on 'The Right to Life and Work': 'All human rights, social, economic, political and religious are inter-related' (also geographically inter-related) and 'are to be taken as a whole and each of the same importance.' Of the *same* importance?

(*b*) Report of Section V of the Nairobi Assembly of the World Council of Churches 1975 (paragraph 19), 'No rights are possible without the basic guarantees for life, including the right to work.' *No* rights without the right to work?

The right to work

1. A good deal of the discussion of this turns into a general reflection of the need for social justice. It needs to be examined more precisely, but when this is done the concept is found to be undeveloped.

2. The concept has been thought of against an urban and industrial background. What of the vast peasant masses in the Third (or Fourth) World who are *condemned* to hard, physical toil – including much child labour – in order to survive? I am not competent to discuss this, but it must be on the agenda.

3. In the industrial world it needs to be put into the immediate context of the increasingly rapid phasing out of dead-end physical and mental jobs, and a growingly service economy. Questions of continuing or lower rates of economic growth or a zero rate, or an actual reduction in economic levels lie at one remove from the immediate context.

4. Some comments and queries on this undeveloped concept of the right to work.

(a) It is clearly contrary to a *laissez-faire* view of the state; that could go as far as a minimum subsistence level (as Milton Friedmann does) but not as far as a right to work. There has been a recrudescence of this 'thin' theory of the state recently.

(b) The right to a free choice of work is equally contrary to the centralized 'command' economy (as distinct from a 'market' economy) of the Marxist-Socialist type. Can this right be absolute? Everyone can be kept at work by employing some on unnecessary jobs, and by direction.

(c) Can there be a right to a *particular* job? Here personal and community interests can clash. Everyone wants to keep his own job and resists change when his skills become out of date, especially if a long training or apprenticeship has been involved. Yet resources are scarce compared with their possible uses, and the community must have *some* interest in maximizing their use, otherwise jobs are perpetuated for their own sake regardless of their necessity. How can the community prevent particular individuals having to bear an unfair burden of adjustment to technological and social change?

(d) How far is it a question of the right to be wanted, to have one's personal qualities (whether little or much) recognized, used and paid for? What are we doing when we treat the unskilled as unwanted? Yet there are large numbers of service jobs requiring basic human qualities which the community could benefit from, but it is reluctant to pay for them; instead it pays people a social security allowance to be unemployed.

(e) There is no value in mental or physical drudgery for its own sake. Maybe we should be less work and more leisure orientated – but not the enforced leisure of a minority whom the rest are prone fairly quickly to dismiss as 'scroungers'.

The rights of migrant workers

1. This is a phenomenon found all over the world and has attracted the concerned attention of church and other international bodies. The World Council of Churches has the Churches' Committee on Migrant Workers, and there are national ones in

e.g., Australia, New Zealand, France, Germany, Italy and many others. There are ILO and UNESCO Conventions; and a UN resolution of February 1977 on 'Measures to improve the situation and ensure the Human Rights and dignity of all Migrant Workers'. The phenomenon is connected with questions of economic growth, but in the first instance needs to be addressed directly.

2. In Europe there are variously reckoned to be between eight and twelve million migrant workers. They constitute a foreign sub-proletariat. Few have a vote; many are separated from their families; and trade unions are apt to be wary of them. Migrant women, some trained (like nurses) and others with little formal education, are a special aspect. In addition there are thought to be half a million illegal immigrants in Europe drawn to where they are to escape the poverty at home. Since the churches must have a special concern for the poor and disadvantaged it is no wonder that migrant workers have claimed their attention.

3. The attitude of host countries is ambivalent. Migrant labour is welcomed to fill unfilled jobs when the economy is flourishing; it is fairly easy to shed in a recession; and capital invested at home is more secure than it would be in migrants' countries. Yet there are also periodical xenophobic anti-immigrant backlashes.

4. Should the church fight the whole immigrant worker system? Some allege that it should on the grounds (a) that it holds back needed structural changes in both the receiving and the home country; (b) migrant workers are badly treated as 'guest workers', and don't fit when they finally return home; (c) we should push on the economic development of the home countries. By themselves these points may be too simple. Even if they were implemented, the idea of everyone working within relatively closed national boundaries is an odd one in view of international interdependence in a 'global village'.

5. Assuming the system continues, what should be done?

(a) Helping migrant workers to organize themselves in trade unions; pressing for improved training schemes; and in general breaking away from 'paternalistic' care.

(b) Urging that they should enjoy human rights at the level they exist in the receiving country; that they should be regarded as citizens, together with the right to their own community cultural institutions etc.

(c) In the case of illegal immigrants, those who employ them should be penalized, and they themselves guaranteed immunity so that they will not be afraid to reveal exploitation.

6. In this connection it should be noted that the Declaration of the Helsinki Conference of 1975 refers to them; and that in 1977 the Council of Europe adopted a European Convention on the Legal Status of Migrant Workers which is now open for ratification. It applies to nationals of any of the countries involved in the Convention (but not to seasonal workers) and provides –

(a) If a migrant worker loses his job he can remain for not less than five months to look for another.

(b) He can bring his family to join him after twelve months.

(c) There are legal procedures for appeal if his residence permit is withdrawn. This is some way behind the points made in (5) above, partly because it contains some hedging reservations, and also because –

   (i) It applies only to salaried employment (one cannot be self-employed).

   (ii) The right to work is restricted.

   (iii) The freedom to form trade unions is only optional.

10

Church and Class

Dr E. R. Norman, the Dean of Peterhouse, Cambridge, has written a study, *Church and Society in England, 1770–1970*, which in its scale, price and point of view alike make its publication a major event.[1] It requires a careful appraisal. True it covers a fairly well-tilled field. Yet because of its well chosen restriction of topics it can go into more detail on those it covers than can more general English church histories of the nineteenth and twentieth centuries. Also it is largely confined to the Church of England, and within that church it concentrates on issues of church and state, church and politics, law and public morality, and to a much lesser extent on education. The sources are mainly episcopal charges, speeches at church congresses, reports of Lambeth Conferences, convocations, church boards, pamphlets, and collections of papers of some outstanding bishops, together with a very wide range of historical, biographical, and to some extent theological and sociological, writing. It is concerned with church leaders, mainly clerical, representative church bodies, and particular organized church groups.

The point of view is explicit. Dr Norman sets out to correct what he considers erroneous and even dangerous received opinions. At times the tone is that of a polemical tract. However the reader is given a clear indication of the point of view in the introduction, the conclusions are not left to the end, so that he knows exactly where he is and can weigh matters for himself.

Dr Norman's thesis begins with the point that the church was faced with an unprecedented rate of social change in this period, for which population and economic growth can serve as examples, with which she never caught up. This is familiar. He goes on to maintain that the clergy gave little thought to social and political morality because they had little instruction in it. Roman Catholic priests, by contrast, were trained in seminaries where systematic teaching in moral theology survived. Priests of the Church of England, however, were related by class and culture to the ruling professional sections of society; they could be said to be 'gentlemen' in holy orders, though this is not a phrase used by Dr Norman. The Englishman's Erastian approach to religion demanded that the parson keep out of politics, and the continuity of English political institutions ensured that the church never had to take sides in a clash of political ideologies. So far we are not conscious of any new perspectives, and are grateful for a refreshing frankness which is not afraid to face social and class facts.

Dr Norman goes on to say that the church avoided partisan politics (I think he means party politics) from the end of the eighteenth century, or the endorsing of particular political forms of government or social organization but that this was obscured in the latter part of the nineteenth century by disputes over establishment, provoked by dissent, which drove the church into supporting the Tory party. In general the social attitudes of the church derived from the current intellectual and social assumptions and not, as many churchmen liked to think, from theological reflection. The social ethic expressed was a class ethic, and that class was not the working class. The church had never been *en rapport* with it. Workers did not go to church in the villages from which they came into the growing urban areas (no evidence is offered on this), and they did not go when they arrived there. New churches built for them were more than half empty. The middle and upper classes interpreted this refusal to go to church as a sign of atheism and immorality, likely to lead to revolution and anarchy, but it was not a sign of unbelief but of the fact that they associated the church with the upper classes. Their general attitudes were morally and politically conservative. So far we remain on familiar ground. The phenomenon of the working-class Tory, especially the women, is well known. At least one-third of what are usually thought of as working class people must always vote Tory or we should have nothing but Labour governments.

Now we come to the polemical part of the thesis. The clergy had upper middle class assumptions and standards of living. But some among them took 'progressive' or 'radical' attitudes instead of resting within the general social ethic of their class.

They are charged with following the changing intellectual fashions of the liberal intelligentsia, and indulging in a moralism which was just as much class based as that of the rest of their class. The social composition of the clergy did not change much (no evidence is offered on this), and the radicals were no more capable of transcending class attitudes and culture than the rest, though they had the illusion that they did. In fact they were just as alien to the workers. Amusing instances are quoted. Fives was the game popular among the staff of Oxford House Settlement in Bethnal Green. When the church Congress decided that it should have a meeting for workers it was put on a week-day afternoon, and at it bishops spoke of themselves as workers before driving back to their palaces. The parochial clergy and laity were much more uniformly conservative, and were only making a start in catching up with the progressive element among the church leaders when many of those leaders turned to the next fashion of the liberal intelligentsia, so the two groups remained out of step. The progressives among the leaders adopted the new *laissez-faire* theories whilst the local clergy clung to a more organic and paternalist view, disapproving of the socially disruptive effects of *laissez-faire* doctrines as preached and practised by Dissenting manufacturers. Just as these views began to be eroded by *laissez-faire* ones, the progressive clerical leaders swung over to collectivism.

It is this which is Dr Norman's bugbear. He realizes, as advocates of *laissez-faire* came to do, that some particular modifications of the hostility to state action were necessary, partly in the common interest (epidemics of cholera were a powerful solvent of pure *laissez-faire* theories), and partly on humanitarian grounds to help those who could not help themselves. It is an over-all theory of state action which he deplores. As the book gets nearer to the present time it becomes less of a history and more of a polemical tract. The style, level of discussion and point of view remind one most of the anonymous prefaces to *Crockford's Clerical Directory*. The other author who most comes to mind is Bishop Hensley Henson, who does in fact figure prominently in the book, almost always with approval. Dr Norman has something of the independent mind, the mordant style, the insight, the exposure of humbug and the frequent perversity of interpretation which is associated with that great man. Dr Norman calls him a Gladstonian Liberal, a term which would not be altogether inappropriate if applied to Dr Norman himself. A third author who frequently appears, and always with approval, is Professor V. A. Demant, though it is doubtful whether Dr Norman has come to grips with what Dr Demant has primarily been concerned to say about church and society; what earns his approval is that Dr Demant has tried to bring a theological critique to bear on society and not to echo current 'progressive' orthodoxies.

As the book proceeds and becomes more polemical it appears that three things in particular annoy Dr Norman.

1. Sloppy thinking; in particular the habit of using terms like 'brotherhood' or 'fellowship' without any serious analysis of how they could work out in economic institutions. This he holds to have been particularly characteristic of the Christian Social Union, a body run by upper-class clergymen who expressed a moralizing sympathy for the workers, which lacked hard thought and spread around an air of benevolent unreality. This is a criticism which I have made myself ever since I began to become informed in these matters, and to my mind Dr Norman vindicates his case.

2. Dissent; this receives very short shrift from such an establishment man. Dissent was no more free from folly than the Church of England during these years, but Dr Norman shows no insight into the way the attitudes, culture and position of the church appeared to very large elements in the nation who had dissented from it ever since 1662.

3. The attitude of so many 'progressive' Christians, from the time of the Christian Social Union onwards, to their immediate forebears; it was alleged that they were not concerned with social ethics, and at the most got no further than the need for social 'ambulance work'. Temple, for one, often spoke in this way. Dr Norman maintains that *laissez-faire* attitudes were not an attempt to remove ethics from economic life, but in the minds of those Christians who argued for them it was an attempt to bring ethics to bear on economic life. Political economy, of which *laissez-faire* was the expression, was thought of as a 'science' and therefore following economic laws was to them following the divine creation.

This point may be accepted but its implications are devastating. How could thoughtful Christian men come to think of a *laissez-faire* theory as an overall theory of man in society, whereby God ensures that the good of the whole will be secured by each following his own self-interest? At best it is a limited theory of how, given strong underlying social and political institutions, a fair range of production and distribution can conveniently be organized on the basis of a free market instead of by collective decisions. How could such a theory take such a hold as an over-all interpretation of economic life? How could good Christian men be so attached to such an orthodoxy that in good conscience they could behave as they did to the Irish at the time of the potato famine of 1846? It is explicable only because of the collapse of the tradition of Christian social teaching at the end of the seventeenth century. Richard Baxter was the last well-known exponent of it. Why it collapsed, and how far the collapse was its own fault are questions it is impossible to examine now. But that it had collapsed is clear. This point, made by R. H. Tawney and William Temple and many others, can surely not be denied. By the year Dr Norman's book starts there had been a century of vacuity in Christian social ethics. There was no living tradition on which to draw. The limitations of such a vigorous and thoughtful man as John Wesley in this area are evidence of it. No one who had been schooled in the traditions of Christian social ethics would have been taken in by the pretensions of *laissez-faire* theory. What the church was left with at the beginning of the vast social change set in motion by the Industrial Revolution, was an uncritical assumption that the existing social order was ordained by God, an individualistic doctrine of stewardship, and an attenuated doctrine of personal charity; attenuated because of the division made between the deserving and the undeserving poor and the fear of undermining the character and independence of the former.

On all this Dr Norman is silent. Indeed it is strange that having given a devastating analysis of the class ethic taught by Church of England clergymen, he can do no more than round on those of them who criticized this as sentimental, class guilt-ridden moralists. A very diverse lot of people are put in this category including, readers will be astonished to note, Bishop Stephen Neill. What does Dr Norman want? What is his own ideal? He does not give us many clues. One is at the end of the introduction where we are reminded of Archbishop Summers' remark that 'men, in every state, are less inclined to change of habits by reason, than by example', and we are told that this is what the parishes of the land have silently witnessed to during the last two centuries. It is a claim which is as baffling to make as to substantiate. For one thing there was much vocal in the witness; little in this book encourages me to be happy about the social ethics it spoke of. And what of the silence? We know something, for example, of the silent witness of the little Brothers and Sisters of the Poor as they identify themselves with the poor and oppressed. How many similar, or any other kind of, silent examples were given through the Church of England? And if we are thinking of the devout member of the Church of England who attends his parish church but is inarticulate and silent about his faith, what exactly is the witness he was giving during this period in social ethics (as distinct from personal integrity and charity) which is the subject of this book? Earlier in the introduction it is said that the pursuit of eternity is the first preoccupation of organized religion. This bifurcation is revealing for it suggests that in some way the pursuit of eternity can be separate from, and prior to, the witness to the eternal given by the attitudes to society in the church and the structures of the church itself. This is an attitude frequently taken, but it subtly demotes the things of this world. Perhaps this is the reason Dr Norman seems to be happy with a church that endorsed accepted institutions and is uneasy with those who wished to change them. It is surprisingly difficult to do justice both to time and eternity, to the love for God and the love for man, and perhaps few Christians manage it. One of the most successful contemporary examples of the ability to do this is the Taizé Community in the French Reformed Church, and that is why its appeal to the young is so encouraging.

Dr Norman also sets great store by the doctrine of original sin. Indeed the only theological episode in recent history which wins his condemnation is the time immediately before, during and after the Second World War, when theologians made great play with it under the influence of biblical theology and what Karl Barth was supposed to stand for. The doctrine is unfortunately named, as unfortunate as Natural Law, so that it is widely misunderstood. Reinhold Niebuhr, in whose thought it played a large part (as did original righteousness), gave up using the term because of the endemic misunderstanding it caused among his readers. Nevertheless properly understood it is important. However, Dr Norman seems to assume that it leads to a conservative rather than a radical stance. It has usually done so, but it need not. It can lead to either. What it does is to call into question all utopianism. For the rest it can lead to a critical attitude to those in power and not only to elements of woolly idealism in those who would replace them. Used superficially, however, it can easily lead to an irresponsible attitude, dismissing both conservative and radical from a supposed independent position of a lofty concern for eternity, and ignoring what precisely is the witness which is being given by the organized structures of the church, as well as by the personal attitudes of Christians. In practice this amounts to a particularly irresponsible, because silent and not thought out, support for things as they are. In any case original sin is not the only Christian doctrine, nor the chief. In his zeal to maintain that they echoed the opinions of the liberal intelligentsia Dr Norman does not do justice to the place of the doctrine of the incarnation in the thinking of the many 'progressives' whom he criticizes.

Above all, Dr Norman, as we have seen, is an establishment man. The National Church means a great deal to him. He puts a great deal of weight on the non-church going, inchoate, diluted religion of the worker, whose attitudes are basically those of the more church going, middle and upper classes (apart from the guilt-ridden and sentimental 'progressives' among them). At bottom they all stand for the unity of religion and civil society, which is expressed by the National Church in so far as it was not spoiled by the superficial and inconsistent protests by Dissent. Indeed to differentiate Christian from public attitudes is a sectarian undertaking. To state this explicitly is to reveal its implausibility, especially as applied to this century. What exactly this English working-class religion amounted to in the last century and amounts to now has been the subject of a fair amount of investigation by historians and sociologists of religion, but Dr Norman does not discuss this. But his assumptions about the establishment mean that he does not appear to object to arguments used to defend the Church of England which fill one with depression. The cause of God and the financial, political and educational position of the church seem to be totally equated. The harm this did, for instance in education, could in fact be illustrated from Dr Norman's own sphere of university education.

His assumptions become harder and harder to sustain as we approach 1970, the terminus of the book, and the fact that we live in a plural society becomes more obvious. Dr Norman abhors such a society as inherently unstable; in his view only the intelligentsia is inclined to pluralism and only it has the illusion that it is happening. These attitudes give an air of archaism to his treatment of the moral and social issues on which church leaders and groups have written and spoken in recent decades, so that one is driven to say with respect to the last two chapters, from 1940 onwards, that he often simply does not understand what the issues are. Occasionally his judgments strike me as ludicrous; for example, that the reason why the British clergy thought British Fascism alien and were never sympathetic to it, was that it lacked the leadership by a section of the bourgeois intelligentsia that socialism had. The grain of truth here is as nothing to the error.

At bottom, Dr Norman appears to have in his mind a picture of a National Church, bound up with the predominant attitudes and *mores* of its time, suspicious on theological grounds of reformers and radicals, confining itself to stating general principles for society, whilst predominantly pointing men and women to eternity. Further, he sets great store by what he considers the common assumptions of English laymen about religion. But can their attitudes be a criterion? Are they exempt from original sin? It would be absurd to reject this altogether, but it is surely a seriously inadequate basis for an historical investigation of church and society. I do not understand how this basis is to be reconciled with the statement that the church never caught up with the rapid social changes in the period covered, but that is because there are so few indications of what attitudes Dr Norman would approve of. I suspect that his desiderata are not consistent. Be that as it may one can learn much from an author even if his point of view seems unsound, especially from a major work by a professional historian. The early part seems to me well researched, the later part less so. I was much interested in the efforts of the English clergy to help exiled French Roman Catholic priests at the time of the Revolution, something which was new to me. Sometimes where the subject was familiar to me I found Dr Norman unsatisfying. Take the case of F. D. Maurice and the Christian Socialists. Some sharp points are made about their class attitudes and their paternalism. They began by opposing Chartism, which was a working-class movement, though they made several contributions to the growth of the later working-class movement which is ignored. Maurice himself is described as a classical bourgeois utopian with an element of jingoism in him. The attack is effective against a sentimentalized view of him, but no impression is given of the place of the doctrine of the incarnation in Maurice's thought, nor of the long-term significance of Producers' Co-operatives, which Maurice hit on, as one alternative method of economic organization.

In the later parts the polemical aims of the book tend to get in the way of the exposition, and reservations grow. Here are some examples briefly noted.

1. The Christendom Group is called Christian Socialist, something it was increasingly concerned to deny. And Bishop David Sheppard will be astonished to find himself classed with them.

2. Liberal Christianity is said to go with radical social ethics. That was not my experience of The Modern Churchmen's Union and its conferences. Most social and political attitudes were found within it, but the dominant was bourgeois Tory.

3. References to the ecumenical movement are few but dismissive. The only explicit evidence quoted is to the Uppsala Assembly, and then not to any actual speech or report, but to a remark made on it subsequently in a minor British book.

4. The question of homosexuality is introduced by the phrase homosexual *misconduct*, which prejudices the discussion from the start.

5. No one could get an idea of the ethical issues involved in the situation ethic debate from the discussion of it here. It is dismissed as an ethic of leisure for those who live life second hand, and to that absurdity is added the remark that it is unsuitable for a sheet-metal worker.

6. Mr Don Cupitt is alleged to have written that original sin is now discredited because of our present knowledge of human sexual reproduction, but on looking up the reference given one finds that Mr Cupitt says no such thing.

7. The church is accused of not taking up industrial issues which are of concern to workers yet there is no mention of the growth of industrial 'missioners' which has been so marked since 1945.

8. A favourite condemnatory term is 'moralistic', but it is far from clear what it means. At times it appears to mean ignoring that politics is about power; it is said that the Christendon Group was moralistic about the state because it ignored this. Yet we are told that issues of race, 'Third World' development, minority rights, censorship and sexual liberation are moralistic. Again the idea that everyone should be involved in the great issues of the day is said to be moralistic. I am baffled.

One could go on. The book fascinates and provokes, and

leads one to take copious notes. If one knows something about the matter one can gain a good deal from it, but it is not serviceable for those who do not. The bibliography is full and useful. One or two books that I think well of are not mentioned, but that is a small matter. But I cannot help thinking that it is a pity that nothing of Reinhold Niebuhr is included, if only because of his influence on William Temple; and that Richard Niebuhr's *Christ and Culture* is missing, because its typology might have clarified Dr Norman's ideas on how he would wish church and society to be related.

Dr Norman paradoxically uses the sharp language of class, largely Marxist in origin, apparently to uphold the existence of basic agreement in society, underlying class attitudes, except for the 'progressive' intelligentsia. He may well be indicating something important, but he surely dismisses conflicts too easily. I would draw the opposite conclusion to him from his devastating class analysis of the attitudes of the clergy of the Church of England, namely the need to encourage all those sources of renewal in the Christian tradition which mitigate the tendency of the church to sacralize the *status quo* uncritically. There is plenty of room in the Christian church for critical conservatives but not for uncritical ones, still less for those who unthinkingly support the *status quo* under the guise of being 'non political'. Too simple an identification with the existing class structure has been the continual temptation of the Church of England. It led to archaism in the days of Charles I and Laud with disastrous results for the church. It happened again as the Industrial Revolution got under way. The Christian faith is always in search of a cultural and social expression, as A. N. Whitehead said it is of a metaphysical one, and it can never settle down in any. It has to respond to secular change but not follow it uncritically. There is nothing in itself sinister in church leaders being influenced by 'progressive' elements in the intelligentsia among whom they move. It is only sinister if they respond uncritically. Indeed Christian ethical thinking can only be done in reflection with the most responsible thinking of its time. The church needs to facilitate such common reflection, partly in order that its own leaders may be properly briefed. Changing circumstances and changing knowledge put questions to theology, and theology asks questions of current attitudes, and often points to deeper issues. There is a reciprocal relationship between the two. Sometimes church leaders do take up fashionable nostrums uncritically. On the other hand they and theologians have often been forced to change traditional opinions by the weight of new empirical evidence. These points could be abundantly illustrated from the period with which Dr Norman deals, and it is his inability to see them which makes his treatment so unsatisfactory.

Two things stand out as desirable from reading this book. One is for a much more sociologically sophisticated study of the working of the church as an institution; the recent revival of the sociology of religion is making a contribution to this. The other is the old problem of the relation of the church to the worker. The unconscious class attitude of the 'progressives' are exposed. On the other hand George Orwell's challenge to the bourgeois that they have nothing to lose but their aitches is no better. Those who started the Sheffield Industrial Mission, a pioneer, thought that the gulf was so great that we might have to put up with parallel churches for a couple of generations.

A last point is that Dr Norman polarizes the situation for the church as either staying with general principles or becoming involved in party politics. But this is surely much too simple. There are many steps between these two positions which are not reflected in this book. Space is lacking to tell of them. Indeed much of the work of the ecumenical movement in Christian social ethics has been concerned with just this middle realm, and our understanding of the best ways of carrying on Christian ethical reflection has become much greater through it. No one could guess this from Dr Norman's scattered and disparaging references. Nor would anyone guess that in its early days, in the traumatic decade of totalitarianism and mass unemployment, the theological work put by the ecumenical movement into the Oxford Conference on 'Church, Community and State' in 1937 matched and indeed outpassed the best secular, political and social analysis of the time. The study of church and society in England need not be insular.

It is true that the continuity of British institutions has meant that the church has not been compelled to take sides in an ideological confrontation. Perhaps that is why we have found it so hard to understand situations in the world, reflected in the ecumenical movement, where this immunity has not been possible. We cannot presume that the British situation will last for ever. If it can last it will be a blessing, for it may make orderly social change to a more just and humane society easier. But if a continuity and agreement is to be promoted it will not be by underplaying social conflicts but by facing them creatively. One way of helping this on is for the church to free itself from the overwhelmingly middle and upper class attitudes reflected in this book, to relate itself more effectively to different groups in our plural society, and to study to promote the right kind of social change, and in time. In this way the radical will be the best conservative.

11

Towards Transnational Social Ethics?

Introductory comments

1. As we all know the literature on Transnational Companies (TNCs) has grown enormously in the 1970s; apart from the large number of books anyone who tries to keep abreast of the discussions soon finds his file of significant cuttings overflowing. The check in this decade to the steady economic advance of the West which occurred in the two previous decades has produced an atmosphere of criticism of the working of our industrial and economic and political institutions, and among these TNCs are a large and obvious target. Moreover there have been a number of scandals involving them which has intensified public scrutiny.

2. The churches have inevitably been drawn into this discussion. It is true that they might adopt an 'otherworldly' gospel (as some Christian groups have always done in Christian history), but such an attitude has not been characteristic of any of the main Christian confessions, which have always felt some responsibility for things of this world and not merely for preparing for the next. In an important sense, therefore, this changing world provides the agenda for the churches though not, of course, the criteria for dealing with it. That is why the churches have been drawn into the current debates on our political economic and industrial institutions, including the role of TNCs. For instance the World Council of Churches is holding an international conference at Massachusetts Institute of Technology in July of this year on the theme 'Faith, Science and the Future', with a subsidiary theme, 'A Just, Participatory and Sustainable Society'. I shall refer to this later.

3. It is not surprising that respresentatives of TNCs, including Christian business executives, are often critical of church investigations and criticism. No one likes being criticized. Also the critics may not themselves have examined the issues thoroughly enough. Moreover it seems that business executives are not clear on the basis from which these church investigations and criticisms start, nor on the methods by which they proceed. Therefore I shall do my best to answer in the brief space available the three questions raised on these matters in the 'Notes on the Theme' circulated beforehand by UNIAPAC to all participants in this consultation and dated November, 1978.

Question 1   What are the biblical and theological foundations of these studies and these dialogues? How is the teaching of the churches evolving?

4. To begin with we must note that two main traditional grounds for Christian moral thinking have lost their stability – the Bible and Natural Law. (The other two are claims by individual Christians to direct personal divine inspiration, and by church bodies to utter authentic dogmatic moral teaching on detailed and specific ethical issues; in the space available I cannot deal with them, except to say that in my view they are also called into question, though in different ways.) As to the Bible, the growth of historical criticism has overwhelmed biblical literalism but its ghost still lingers in the tendency to treat, for example, the New Testament as a store of proof texts. As to Natural Law, whilst it is important to hold on to the concept, in the sense of affirming that the realm of the moral and the making of moral judgments is *natural* to men, the idea that human nature is so fixed that we can specify in detail certain actions as natural and to be followed or unnatural and to be shunned, is no longer tenable. The corollary of both these points is that the idea of an 'omnicompetent church' whose leaders and theologians can issue precise and detailed instructions on conduct, including the social, economic, industrial and political sphere, is no longer cogent. (The 'Christendom' era is over in terms of thought as well as in terms of the political and social power of churches.) This is well brought out in paragraph 43 of the Pastoral Constitution of the Second Vatican Council, *Gaudium et Spes*, which says 'Let the layman not imagine that his pastors are always such experts that to every problem which

arises, however complicated, they can readily give him a concrete solution, or even that such is their mission.'

5. To say all this is not of course to say that Christian social teaching has no biblical or theological foundations, but that they bear on contemporary issues less directly (though profoundly) than has traditionally been thought. For instance the ministry of Jesus in word and deed is the centre of the New Testament, and the heart of this is his understanding of the kingdom or rule of God as being inaugurated in his own mission, and remaining active as leaven in the lump of the world through the community of his most faithful disciples (and yet at the crucial moment also faithless), who after his death became the nucleus of the reconstituted people of God. This has the ongoing task of participating in God's mission to the world of which his mission in the ministry of Jesus is the key. The kingdom or rule of God is highly paradoxical in its nature – it is a kingdom whose king rules by service and suffering not by coercion – and so is the ethic which goes with it. The Sermon on the Mount of Matthew chapters 5–7 is the most succinct expression of it. This is always in search of a social expression and never achieved in any society or institution. It always challenges the *status quo* and calls for a fuller realization. The single word which most adequately sums up this ethic is love (*agape*), and the fullest picture of it is found in St Paul's first letter to the Corinthians, chapter 13. St Paul fully understood Jesus in this crucial matter.

6. St Paul's letters and others in the New Testament give in addition examples of ethical teachings, and warnings and encouragement, on quite specific issues (see, for instance, I Corinthians 7), but these are related to their own time and culture, and these detailed instructions must not be transposed into our situation in the twentieth century without allowing for this. Moreover the early Christians had no public responsibility or position in the state such as we have in our Western democracies today. They also had apocalyptic expectations of the imminent end of time and the return of Christ, and had relatively soon to adjust their outlook when this faded. St John's Gospel shews how this was done. Awareness of the socially and culturally conditioned situation of the earliest Christians makes us realize that social and cultural factors affect our understanding today. We can be partially aware of these and allow for them,

but not totally aware. This is why we realize that the Bible cannot be used in the old way.

7. The earliest Christians in the course of time embodied their oral teaching about Jesus into written gospels and combined these with a selection of occasional writings into a collection of books which they recognized as authoritative and which we call the New Testament. They also thought out the implications of their worship of Jesus in a Trinitarian doctrine of God. Christians today are the heirs of both these developments and in them are the roots of the Christian social ethic, whether it be concerned with TNCs or any other matter. Putting it very briefly we can say that Christians believe in (*i*) God who as creator is actively involved in the world in nature and history, where human beings made in his 'image' are to be found and who are intended by him for eternal life with him and one another in him; (*ii*) God the redeemer or restorer who has brought into being a community – the church – of those who are being radically renewed in responding to his kingly rule, and having become aware through Jesus the Christ of what is the divine plan for mankind are joyfully responding to it; (*iii*) God the sanctifier or strengthener who does not leave himself without some witness in the heart of every person in every land. The whole activity of God – Father, Son and Holy Spirit – towards the world is to humanize it; to make it a sphere where true humanity flourishes.

8. From this basic but general biblical and theological foundation it is possible to see that certain general requirements for human flourishing follow. For example freedom, justice as fairness and fellowship (or, in the language of the French Revolution, liberty, equality and fraternity). But (*i*) putting detailed content into these concepts is notoriously difficult; (*ii*) none of them can be taken to the limit without coming into conflict with the others; (*iii*) the right balance between them at any given time is not at all easy to achieve. Nevertheless they all have to be brought to bear upon specific issues at specific times.

9. There is no way of moving directly from either the Bible or theology to specific issues without examining the data of a specific situation. The method of doing this is by dialogue and consultation. The moral theologian cannot do it on his own. He must be associated with those who have direct and relevant experience of what is in question. This applies to the question of TNCs and the ethical problem to which they give rise. The

consultations may be with Christians, as in a UNIAPAC symposium, or with experts – whether Christian or not – whose expertise is a useful contribution to the study, or with adherents of other faiths and ideologies, or with all three. There are many difficulties and uncertainties in this process; getting all the relevant evidence; sifting it and deciding what weight to give to different elements in it; and making some judgment when the experts differ, as they frequently do. The process is as untidy as life itself. It is foolish to think that ethical problems are simple, or that there can be only one answer to them.

10. To answer the last part of the question, (How is the teaching of the churches evolving?) I should say:

(*a*) They have a more positive sense of the human possibilities in human history, under God, than in the more static pre-industrial past; at the same time they are suspicious of utopian hopes because they have a strong sense of the follies and sins of men, as well as of their great potentialities, and do not think that the inhumanities men do to men is only due to oppressive and unjust social structures and will disappear when they are removed.

(*b*) On the whole they have a positive attitude to the freeing of human life and institutions from ecclesiastical control. They do not regard human creativity and man's increased power over his own life and environment as a diminution of God's power. At the same time they are aware that human pride leads easily to the misuse of power, and that this is a danger that goes with the continued development of applied science and technology. In particular man in his pride may blunder in the universe by not studying nature carefully enough and thus creating disastrous side effects which he could have foreseen.

(*c*) They are increasingly aware of the necessity for joint work in social ethics (cf. par. 9 above), realizing that fact, interpretation and evaluation are closely connected.

(*d*) They are increasingly aware of the plural nature of modern society (nationally and globally), and that God wills the flourishing of all mankind whether or not in the first place men and women are Christians. So Christians have a responsibility for, and need an ethic at the level of, common humanity.

(*e*) The thought of the church as a servant (as Jesus came to serve and not be served), and of the people of God as on a

pilgrimage under God with all mankind has grown markedly, though its institutional expression lags behind. Traditional hierarchical structures are powerful.

(*f*) The need to 'ideologize' (in the sense of helping men to
formulate forward-looking goals), is stressed, at the same
time as the need to criticize ideologies (in the sense of
over-all interpretations of life) for the dangerous intellectual
and political pretensions they exhibit. Under God Christians
are hopeful for the human future, but they know less about
it than current political ideologies claim to know.

11. In setting down these points I am conscious that they
give the impression that the churches are more confident than
is in fact the case. In practice they are often timid when they
realize the erosion of their past ethical bases (cf. par. 4ff.), and
the complexities and uncertainties which open out before them.
In particular they are afraid that becoming involved in specific
issues will lead to disagreements and upset the fellowship of
believers. They are tempted to try to take neutral positions *au
dessus de la mêleé*, which on closer examination proves to be
impossible and a deception. In terms of the Protestant tradition
they need to take firmer hold on the Lutheran emphasis on the
continued outpouring of God's love on men and women who
do not deserve it and cannot earn it, because they are always
simul justus et peccator (at the same time forgiven and sinners),
and on the Calvinist doctrine on the certainty of God's election,
though based on his love rather than his sovereignty, as in
Calvin himself. Together they prevent a fear of falling out of
grace because of faulty political and economic diagnoses and
choices, and also give resources for holding together in fellowship Christians who may conscientiously take different political
and economic stances from one another, or from one which the
church as such may feel compelled to take when she realizes
that a neutral position on some issues is impossible.

*Question 2   How far are these biblical and theological foundations
interpreted by different groups? How can the fact be understood
that sometimes the conclusions of these groups present
differences? How can listening and dialogue be promoted, both
of which are essential conditions for coherent action?*

12. There have always been different theological emphases
in the church, and this is reflected in the New Testament itself.

In the course of Christian history these differences hardened into confessional structures which still dominate the scene. But the change from a relatively static to a rapidly changing world has produced a spectrum of theological positions within each confessional tradition. In large measure confessional divisions no longer correspond to theological realities. In social ethics there has been a remarkable general convergence between the teaching of the most recent papal encyclicals etc., (but not *Humanae Vitae*) and that of ecumenical conferences and consultations of the World Council of Churches. It is impressive that there is so much general consensus in the diagnosis of our time. But this does not mean that there are no differences within and between them, and that there are not strongly expressed minority positions. For instance those Christians who think that nothing less than the radical transformation of the entire economic system of Western social democracies is required will be radical critics of TNCs as a major feature of what they want to overthrow. We must abandon any idea of expecting monolithic Christian social teaching, whilst being prepared to take very seriously any provisional and general consensus which may emerge.

13. Reasons for different conclusions in social ethics may therefore arise from different basic theological interpretations, though I think this is less likely among those influenced by the ecumenical movement than has been the case in the past. More likely reasons for different interpretations include:

(a) Situations differ. At the moment it is very difficult for Christians from the First and Third Worlds to see things in the same way; in particular the continuing economic power of the First World is such that it is hard for anything it does to be viewed favourably by the Third World.

(b) Interpretation of the evidence may differ, and different weightage be given by different individuals and groups to the same 'facts', even if these facts are agreed on, which is by no means always the case. Even statistics are notoriously difficult to interpret (hence the English saying which refers to lies, damned lies and statistics). The aim of a corporate investigation into a problem of social ethics is to come to an understanding of the main facts and trends in a situation, assess their significance, and indicate the general direction in which it is desirable that change may be fostered. This is a middle level between general principles (like liberty, equality and fraternity) and detailed policies. It is unlikely that a consensus will get as far as detailed policies. It may not be possible to get as far as this. In such a case all that can be achieved is to establish if possible an agreed analysis, and then list the questions that Christians who advocate one type of policy wish to ask those who advocate a different one, and urge each group to take seriously the questions posed to them by fellow Christians who disagree with them, and not to lose their common togetherness in Christ because of tensions caused by their differences. This has happened in the case of those Christians who take a pacifist position which abjures all violence in principle and those who do not rule it out in all circumstances (e.g., the World Council of Churches' study on 'Violence, Non-Violence and the Struggle for Social Justice').

(c) When it comes to detailed policies for action it is possible that Christians who agree on the middle ground (mentioned in (b) above) may disagree on these in so far as the decision depends on an estimate of the likely consequence of following each of the options for action which are available; no one can be certain of future consequences.

14. The second part of this question asks how listening and dialogue can be promoted, since they are essential to coherent action. They can only be promoted by giving time and resources to them. To bring people into dialogue who normally never do so, either because they are lost in their day-to-day responsibilities or because it has never occurred to them to do so, takes time to arrange (to remove suspicions, win trust and elicit co-operation), time in execution (because those from different backgrounds who normally never discuss together take some time to understand what the others are saying and not misinterpret it), and a catalyst to facilitate the whole process (and this is a skilled job). Such dialogues ought constantly to be happening from the local and congregational level to the international, such as this one. The scope is endless. But the task is not easy. In particular the relation of the churches to the articulate industrial worker has been so poor that there is much mistrust to overcome. The churches do not in fact give much priority in time or resources to the promotion of such dialogues, nor do they give much to the ecumenical movement to do it.

*Question 3   What do the churches' studies contribute in defining
     international problems with which they, as well as
     transnational enterprises, are confronted? How can the
     churches effectively help business executives in their ethical
     research?*

15. The churches' studies are unlikely to draw attention to
international problems which no one else has thought of, but
they may well stress particular ones as sensitive 'pressure
points' from the point of view of human well being as Christians
understand it. For example let us consider the World Council
of Churches' call for a just, participatory and sustainable society.
The call for justice has been perennial; the task is to identify
the most glaring injustices today which need remedying (not a
difficult one). The call for a participatory society is relatively
new. For most of history most people have had little or no say
in the political and economic structures which mould their lives.
Participation in political processes has been achieved in recent
times, notably in Western democracies, but it is patchy, whilst
in industrial structures it has a long way to go. In many countries there are millions on the margin of existence who have
hardly begun to have their say. In the West trade unions have
created power structures among workers which counterbalance
the power of management, and can sometimes be very powerful. In general industrial conflicts are less unequal than they
were, but structures of participation have a long way to go and
raise many problems, not least because consumers and not only
workers need to make their weight felt. The demand for a
sustainable society is a new one and has arisen because of the
recent awareness of the scale on which *known* raw material
resources are being consumed by wealthy countries, and assuming the present level of technological efficiency. Moreover the
need to cope with an increased world population is certain. To
call for a sustainable society seems common sense. However
there are many complications in assessing the dimensions of
the problem, some of it very technical (where again experts can
differ), and not all of it pointing the same way. It is possible to
be carried away by dramatic and alarming slogans which are
ill-founded. Nevertheless there is a sharp warning to wealthy
countries not to blunder about the universe in a short-sighted
way, and to consider much more sharply their responsibilities
to the developing countries.

16. The second part of the question asks how the churches can help business executives in their ethical research. It may seem obvious, but the first thing the church can do for them is to help them to draw more fully on God's resources by public worship, private meditation, and study. It has a pastoral task in helping them to develop a 'spirituality' (to use a traditional term) which makes sense in the contemporary world and is not archaic. In the pressures of life, not least that of business executives, it is very easy either to let worship be crowded out altogether or else to let it be merely an escape from daily preoccupations. For the rest, theology is far too important to be left to the clergy and professional teachers. The aim must be that the Christian layman is himself a 'lay theologian', not in the sense of having degrees and diplomas in theology, but in the sense of so understanding his faith that he will think theologically about his work and the world. The churches have traditionally given a good deal of help in the 'formation' of school teachers in this way, but little to those engaged in industry. It can only be done by co-operative work between pastors, moral theologians, and those earning their living in industry. The same kinds of group work are needed in pursuing specifically 'ethical research' (par. 9ff.), in the hopes that general guidelines may emerge, or at least that the significant questions which ought to be faced are seen more clearly. Such groups should not be confined to fellow business executives (though such a restricted group has its place); it is necessary that those with different experiences of the same problem should listen to one another together with those who are concerned but slightly detached, like the 'secular expert' or the moral theologian.

The question of a transnational social ethic

17. I have deliberately not discussed this directly because many others will do this at the symposium, and I thought that as a theologian I should deal with those questions in the preliminary document specifically put to theologians by Christian business executives who are uneasy about criticisms made by the churches of TNCs. However in conclusion, so as not to avoid the subject entirely, I mention some of the most important questions under this heading as I see them.

(*a*) Questions of power: TNCs are large and powerful. The exercise of power in human life is necessary, but no individual and no group is good enough to exercise power unchecked; countervailing power is needed. The power of shareholders is now very small (even in most cases that of the large institutional shareholder) and so TNCs appear to be self-perpetuating and literally irresponsible organizations. There is also much more secrecy surrounding their operations than there is, for instance, in worker and consumer movements. As I write *The Financial Times* publishes the report of an enquiry into the disclosure habits of big European TNCs with respect to, e.g., group accounts, accounting policies, independent audits and profit forecasts, and some big names come out of it very badly. Secrecy also applies to their internal power structures. How much may even depend on the personal idiosyncracies of the chairman? In a more obvious way TNCs are also powerful agents for social change; how far have they considered their responsibilities for this? I do not know the answer to these questions of power, but they must be faced.

(*b*) Questions of codes of conduct for TNCs. As we know these are much discussed by e.g., the International Chamber of Commerce, the OECD, the UN and the European Trade Union Confederation. It is certainly desirable that ethical insights are structured in codes and conventions (so long as they are flexible enough to be under regular scrutiny). How far should they be voluntary and how far statutory? There is a place for both. Codes are part of the movement to 'professionalize' business management. Professions ensure standards of competence and protect the public against arbitrary behaviour by particular members of the profession. Often the codes are regulated by the profession itself. But the other side of the professions is that they are an organization of a vested interest and can become a conspiracy against the public. If powerful TNCs resist all statutory controls and insist on exclusively voluntary ones the public reaction will be cynical. But how public controls might operate raises many problems. (An interesting half-way example is the British Press Council.)

(*c*) This last point raises questions about the state (nation). We are concerned with *trans*-nationals. If critics want more *national* control, what is their view of the nation-state? Do they accept it as some ultimate unit of government? There is every ground in Christian theology to see the necessity of some basic structure of state authority for human welfare, but none to suggest that each group which thinks of itself as a nation must have a separate national sovereign state. Nationalism is a mixed phenomenon, with some good features and some bad, and is certainly not to be taken uncritically. (The easiest way for the church to be popular is to be nationalistic in each country, a temptation into which it frequently falls.) TNCs may be a partial example of a slow but necessary development of trans-national operations, but the issues raised in point (*a*) above about public accountability have still to be faced. What international institutions are needed to deal with them? Can we expect anything from the EEC in this respect? And in so far as the nation-state is still an appropriate structure, what sort of state should it be? An omnicompetent centralized state with no effective countervailing power could easily become a tyranny.

12

The Next Ten Years in Christian Ethics and Moral Theology

I

A colleague of mine, on hearing that I was about to write an essay on this theme, said that the only thing that could safely be prophesied was that confusion would continue. The remark was intended humorously, but it has a point, and this is that the Christian public in general, still more those to whom it speaks in a pluralist society, has not learned to distinguish between diversity and confusion. In questions of doctrine this is less so, at least as far as the church itself is concerned. The break-up of monolithic confessional doctrinal positions and the wide spectrum of beliefs on doctrinal issues now held within traditional confessional structures is widely acknowledged and lived with, even though there are some in all confessions who yearn for what they see as the old uniformity. The majority, however, accept a variety of doctrinal positions and welcome it, in view of the variety and rapidly changing nature of human situations in which the church is placed, and the fluidity in the different areas of theological scholarship. The breakdown of biblical theology, indeed, has made us more aware of the variety of doctrinal positions in the New Testament from the earliest days of the church. There are obviously elements of confusion within this diversity, and they need to be pointed out, but in general the diversity of doctrinal positions is seen as potentially creative.

In ethics, however, the situation is not so clearly appreciated. In fact, there is as wide a diversity in ethical as in doctrinal positions within the Christian church, both as to methods of proceeding in Christian ethics and as to conclusions on particular issues. However, a lot of Christians are unhappy about this, when they can bring themselves to face it. They think that Christian ethics should arrive at clear moral conclusions, and that those who disagree with those that they themselves have come to are unaccountably misguided. A good deal of this confusion is due to the sheer lack of resources that has been put into Christian ethics, at least in Anglo-Saxon Protestant circles (with the exception of USA), as compared with those devoted, for example, to biblical and doctrinal studies. The result has been that clergy and ministers have been inadequately trained and the laity hardly trained at all in Christian ethics and moral theology. But that is an issue which, although I feel keenly about it, I will not be drawn into discussing now. Suffice it to say that a good deal of work remains to be done in distinguishing differences in method in Christian ethics from inherent possibilities of uncertainty in making specific moral judgments. These are always liable to lead to diversity of conclusions in detail among Christians even if a general consensus on the issue in question is theoretically possible. Until this becomes clear, therefore, we can confidently predict that confusion will continue in Christian ethics. More of what I mean in this abstract statement of the situation will I hope become clearer as this essay proceeds.

Looking ahead is a precarious business, and that for two reasons. The first is the conditioning factors which blinker one's judgment. None of us is able so to transcend his environment, however conscious he is of the need to attempt it, as to take anything approaching a universal position. One of my former students who was involved in the Assembly of the World Council of Churches in Nairobi in 1975 said that the first shock to him was to find that to be a white, male, ordained Anglo-Saxon over thirty was to be in effect written off by many at it. In view of this I must make clear my limitations. I am a white, elderly, ordained priest of the Church of England, wholly English in my antecedents and career, though laced with a lifetime's concern for, and involvement, in the ecumenical movement.

The second element of precariousness in forecasting arises from the fact that it is an inherently conservative activity. One extrapolates from the trends one already identifies, and one is always liable to be subsequently caught out by surprises. This happens in every sphere. I remember saying as a younger man, with complete assurance, that there would not be another Gen-

eral Council in the Roman Catholic Church because the Vatican
Council of 1870 with its declaration on papal infallibility had
made any further general Council otiose. Not only was I completely wrong, still less did I foresee that I would be proved
wrong by an *aggiornamento* instigated by an old man, supposedly a 'caretaker' Pope, John XXIII. In a very different sphere,
but one which in the end influences the church willy nilly by
the social changes it brings about, the case is the same. I refer
to that of technological invention and development. A strong
case can be made for thinking that this is the most powerful
influence in changing human circumstances. Yet it is notoriously difficult to predict the future. H. Kahn and A. J. Weiner, in
their enquiry into *The Year 2000*,[1] refer to a previous effort in
1937 to look ahead which failed to foresee atomic energy, com-
puters, antibiotics, radar and jet propulsion. Methods of forecasting have become more sophisticated since then, but there
is no such thing as a science of 'futurology', and all looking
ahead is liable to be upset by unexpected innovations. In many
pure sciences much of what will be relevant in the year 2000 is
not known at all now, and pure science spills over into applied
science and technology. There is alleged to be a major military
invention every five years (because so much money is spent on
military research), and this leads before very long into applications in civilian life. We are seeing at the moment very rapid
developments in tele-communications and in micro-electronics
(I am thinking of integrated circuits) which may have considerable implications for decentralising decision-making in politics,
economics and industry. For instance, it could mean that a lot
of industry moves from the traditional, heavily-populated, urban industrial areas of the 'north' to less-urban but heavily-
populated areas of the 'south'. This would lead to a diminution
of the powers of the giant multi-national companies. I do not
know what exactly the effects will be, and I may be wrong in
the ones I have mooted, but I am quite sure they will be considerable, and that they will have a lot of influence on the
context within which Christian ethics is done.

There is one more preliminary question to face, the difference
between the terms Christian ethics and moral theology. The
former is usually considered the Protestant term and the latter
the Catholic one, but there is no generally agreed usage, so it
becomes necessary to indicate one's own. Mine derives from
the two fundamental aspects of dealing with an ethical problem;

the first is to act from the right motive and the second is to arrive at the right action in the particular case. If I have to make a distinction between them I always take Christian ethics to refer to the first and moral theology to refer to the second. The first is concerned with the general qualities appropriate to the Christian life. We have seen a lot of work done in this field, for example in exploring the nature of *agape*, ever since the publication in English of Nygren's *Agape and Eros*[2], from 1932–39. In this concern for what Roman Catholics call the 'formation' of character, Christian ethics overlaps with what traditionally has been called ascetical theology. On the other hand, moral theology on this view is concerned with the application of Christian criteria and qualities to specific questions; in short with casuistry. Here we are in trouble straight away because there is a strong strain in Protestantism which denies the validity of the whole enterprise. Protestant pietists assume that if one produces a 'changed', 'converted' or 'consecrated' character that person can safely be left to do what is right without further investigation. In the Lutheran tradition there is also a suspicion of the whole enterprise for fear that the effort to wrestle with the details of particular ethical problems will turn into a justifying work and overthrow the gospel of grace through faith alone. Further, casuistry has not entirely recovered from the bad name it got when its laxity became a weapon in the hands of the Jesuits at the time of the Counter-Reformation. But that was a wrong kind of casuistry. It does not rule out the need for a right kind. This is not the occasion to argue the point. Suffice it to say that to try and live the Christian life like an extemporary speaker is an evasion of half the ethical task of the Christian. There can be no escape from bringing general ethical insights to bear on particular cases, personal and collective. Moral theology in my view is concerned with the best way of doing this. In the last resort everyone has the responsibility of living his own life, no one else can live it for him, and everyone needs to be a casuist. Collective decisions by churches and other Christian bodies also need an appropriate casuistry.

Discernment, which means the use of a disciplined imagination, is needed for both aspects of the ethical task, character formation and the arriving at specific judgments. Fostering this is the concern both of Christian ethics and moral theology. It can be summed up by saying that moral judgment is an art.

II

After these preliminaries I turn to consider where we are now in Christian ethics and moral theology. Then, with all the reservations I have already indicated, I will use my imagination to consider where we may get to in the next ten years. We shall be generally concerned with moral theology rather than Christian ethics, where the chief problems lie. The question of method is basic. Broadly speaking, we have seen a shift from a deductive to an inductive method in moral theology. The deductive method assumed that one could move from a Christian basis, or one acceptable to Christianity, direct to a particular ethical conclusion, by some rule of action derived from the basis. Either no study of particular circumstances and likely consequences was required or at best only enough to characterize the proposed action in order to know what rule it fell under. Casuistry was largely concerned with resolving conflicts of rules. The basis was either the Bible, or the church, or Natural Law (usually as interpreted by the authority of the church). To some extent appeal to the Bible was more characteristic of Protestants and the appeal to the church more characteristic of Catholics, but not entirely. For example, a certain strain in Protestantism condemned gambling as unnatural, and the consensus of the Quaker community practically speaking requires a pacifist position, and that of the Methodist Church until recently ruled out alcoholic drinks. On the other hand, the Roman Catholic Church will adopt an appeal to the Bible where it thinks it can, and is in some difficulty where (as in the case of abortion) it can only do it in a far-fetched way (Ex. 23.7). These sources of authority have broken down in the form in which they were used. Modern critical study of the Bible has made it impossible to take it *tout court* as a source of detailed moral rules, as it has brought out the inadequacies of doing so. The question of divorce among Christians is a good example of this. Those who take an indissolubilist view have considerable difficulties with the letter of the New Testament text (not least the Matthean exception), whilst those who take a dissolubilist view find the letter of the permitted exceptions in the New Testament too narrow for the subtleties of marital breakdown. More important has been the realization of the variety in the Bible, even within the short period covered by the New Testament, and also the necessity of seeing its particular ethical conclusions in their context. St

Paul's teaching on marital questions in I Cor. 7 is only intelligible in the light of his apocalyptic expectation, at that time in his life, of an imminent *parousia*. Even then it is permissable to ask the non-contextual question whether he is right in regarding marriage in the last resort as more of a distraction than celibacy from the single-minded service of God. Similarly, the tendency to rigorism on the one hand and to formalism on the other in the sub-apostolic New Testament writings, so ably dealt with in Kenneth Kirk's *The Vision of God*,[3] needs to be understood against its context if, for instance, we are to cope with the subordinationism in the ethic of the Pastoral Epistles, which has had a most unfortunate influence in the history of Christian ethics and which might well be regarded as the Bible's gift to Marxism. All this presupposes study of the ministry and message of Jesus as received through the witness of the church to it. Central to this is an understanding of the nature of the kingdom of God, realized and future, and its relation to Jesus, and the far-reaching ethic involved in it which transcends any particular culture and society and any complete empirical realization.

The authority of Natural Law, as traditionally used, is also in disarray. I say 'as traditionally used' because St Thomas Aquinas, from whom the tradition chiefly comes, was very cautious in what detailed moral conclusions could be drawn from the concept and well aware of the relative (we might say conditioning) factors involved in doing so. It is his successors who ignored his caution. For instance, he was well aware that monogamy could not be demonstrated on either a biblical or a Natural Law basis. The problem with the common use of Natural Law has been twofold. One is that particular customs of a particular time have been given a permanent status and called 'natural'. St Paul is caught out in this way in I Cor. 11.14f. when, becoming somewhat exasperated with the unruly Corinthians, he says that nature herself teaches us that women have long hair and men short. He thus confuses the customs of his own time with something fixed. He did not know that centuries before him all Homer's heroes were long-haired. What would he have made of the Beatles centuries after him, who initiated a long-haired movement among several generations of young men in the Western world! The other problem with Natural Law is that there has always been the difficulty that what should by definition be known to all who are sane has needed the magisterial authority of the church to point it out. The outstanding recent example is, of course, contraception. Here the papal encyclical *Humanae Vitae* uses three not entirely compatible arguments, but the key one is that contraception is unnatural. This has clearly failed to appear cogent to most thoughtful Christians on the arguments produced, and no better ones have so far been put forward.

Most of the direct moral rules allegedly based on Natural Law are negative ones, and most are in the realm of sex, but not all. Centuries of Christian teaching that usury is unnatural have broken down. The prohibitions are closely related to the idea that certain actions are intrinsically evil, which most people would interpret as meaning of their nature wrong and not to be done in any circumstances. Insofar as this notion depends on the physical nature of an act divorced from any particular human context, it has taken some severe knocks, though attempts are made to rescue the idea. It has particular difficulty in dealing with novelty, whether in the shape of new knowledge about old moral problems or of new problems. Take some examples from sexual ethics. Now we know that some four to six per cent of each sex is congenitally attracted to members of the same sex in the way that the majority is to members of the opposite sex, it is no longer possible to dismiss expressions of that attraction by homosexuals in the traditional way as 'unnatural vice', when it is according to their nature. Some other approach is called for. Or again the entire change in the population situation from the struggle throughout human history to keep it going has resulted (among other factors) in a new look at contraception, sterilization (and even, perhaps, abortion). It has brought relational questions as much to the fore, if not ahead of, procreative ones, and these do not fit so easily into the traditional scheme. On the other hand, new techniques make it possible to help some couples to increase the population who have had difficulty in doing so. When AID (artificial insemination by donor sperm) was a new problem, first heard of after World War II, the reaction was to bring it under the prohibition of adultery (where it still is in law in the UK), but further reflection has shown that to be too simple. When talking of new problems the area of medical ethics should be mentioned, where we are only at the beginning of problems which are arising as a result of the cracking of the genetical code by Crick and Watson in 1953. I do not want to suggest all these ethical problems have achieved clear solutions. There may not indeed be one solution, but a series of considerations which have to be weighed against one another, of different weight in different situations, and more work may well be needed to explore them. But the traditional deductive method in Christian ethics has broken down, whether it be dealing with questions of usury, gambling or sex.

Where in fact did these absolute moral prohibitions come from? Charles Curran, the noted moral theologian of the Catholic University of America, has an interesting essay on this in the symposium *Norm and Context in Christian Ethics*.[4] He maintains that they came mainly from a Christian appropriation of classical thought. Certainly the prohibition of usury was much more based on Aristotle's view that money is barren, that since it does not breed it is wrong to make a charge for it, than on the Old Testament prohibitions (which in any case only applied to fellow Israelites). It also overbore the incidental recognition of the fact of usury by Jesus (Matt. 25.27). It is curious that so much Christian intellectual capital should have gone into a canonization of Aristotle. Curran maintains also that these absolute prohibitions have not been so prominent in Christian history as is often believed. He does not in conclusion say whether there are any, but that in the future the thrust of moral theology will be away from them. This is an interim position of Curran. In later works he has gone further. Other Roman Catholics have said that the only universally prohibited act is blasphemy. Even this can be queried. In any case it is a small harvest from such a long tradition.

The undermining of the authority of the Bible and of Natural Law in ethical matters, as they have most often been used, has in turn made it necessary to think further about the authority of the church in this realm. Roman Catholics, of course, are particularly occupied with the authority of the *magisterium*, but it is a question all confessions have to face. I shall say more about it shortly. Meanwhile I turn to the inductive method in moral theology. By this I mean an approach to the details of an ethical problem by coming to grips with the empirical details of it, especially the human context, and the bringing of them alongside insights derived from the Christian faith. It asks the question, 'What is going on?'. To find out it is necessary to draw upon all those who have relevant experience of the matter in hand. Who these are varies as much as the question which life throws up, and so are the kinds of exploratory groups into which they may be drawn. In some circumstances it merely involves helping one or two people, or a small group, sort out their experience; in others highly technical questions are involved, as in that of the ethics of nuclear energy, where much specialized expertise is necessary. In any case, the moral theologian cannot function by himself. He cannot sit in his study cogitating answers to ethical questions purely from his own resources. He depends upon co-operative work with others, preferably working with them, but in any case using their evidence. If he works with them he may well be a catalyst in the process of group clarification. At a high level of expertise it may be called an inter-disciplinary consultation. The process is inevitably as untidy and varied as life itself.

Several inescapable problems arise. One is the role of experts. We cannot do without them, nor can they be left to settle matters by themselves. Medical ethics is now much too serious and social a matter to be left to the medical profession by itself. Economists can illuminate the parameters of choice and show what is compatible or incompatible with what, but they cannot be left to make social and economic policies by themselves. If we ignore experts or fail to identify who are the real experts from the self-styled ones we can make ourselves look foolish, as did those Christians who uncritically accepted the social credit monetary theories of the engineer Major Douglas in the 1930s. On the other hand, experts differ. Sometimes this is because they have particular explicit or implicit value judgments, or material or intellectual vested interests. Sometimes it is because they are talking beyond their expertise without making this plain, or perhaps realizing what they are doing. Also at the boundaries of any discipline experts differ. Sometimes those whom the experts dismiss as cranks prove right after all. It may not be the case often, but the possibility is there. In the end there is no escape from evaluating evidence, even expert evidence. This is no different in principle in the longer and more complex matters than in the case of illuminating a moral issue which has arisen between two people who see it from different and perhaps irreconcilable points of view. There is always an element of uncertainty in the evaluation, but we must not be paralysed in action or into inactivity by elements of uncertainty. Experience helps and we must be open to learn from it. Sources of help can be drawn upon, not least that of the church. Just as the church can help us in discernment in more personal issues, so it can in more collective ones by organizing the collecting and analysis of evidence at appropriate levels, local, national and international, confessionally or ecumenically (usually more appropriate), and sometimes by joining with non-religious organizations to the same end. If it does this it then has to find the means of bringing what it has done to the notice of its members. Often there is a great weakness at this point. Good work done at a high level never reaches local congregations.

Another difficulty in dealing with expert evidence is that the selection and weightage of 'facts' is always going to have somewhere built into it value judgments in the light of which they are emphasized. In the multitude of facts which occur all the time which are the ones to pick out as significant? And what is their scale of significance? Some principle of selection lies behind the selection. The different sciences isolate their own areas of study and thus abstract from the whole. The 'human sciences' in particular find the thinker more personally involved in what he is studying than do the natural sciences, and there is always some understanding of the nature and significance of human life explicit or implicit in them. In short, 'facts' are seen in a context of significance. The Christian therefore has to be alert to the criteria of significance which lie behind 'expert' studies and evidence. He has his own criteria drawn from the Christian faith, and they may lead to a different selection or weighting of facts from that of others or they may not. Fortunately the different understandings of man are not so completely contradictory that they do not overlap. In particular many forms of humanist view overlap at many points with Christian views. Nor are the chief different religions totally contradictory. If they were, human groups would be so isolated from one another as to make tolerable life together on this planet almost impossible. It is this which makes *some* doctrine of Natural Law possible and necessary, as distinct from those versions of it which have broken down. However, it does mean that the Christian needs to be alert to the criteria behind 'factual' evidence in the social sciences (they have been quicker in the case of psychology), but lately they have taken uncritically evidence in the field of those sciences. The 'limits to growth' arguments were accepted too uncritically by many in the West, whilst in Latin America liberation theologians have accepted too uncritically Marxism's claims to be a science.

In short, the distinction between deductive and inductive methods as I have drawn it so far is too simple. There needs to be a reciprocal relationship between criteria drawn from the Christian faith and evidence drawn from human experience at whatever level up to the most expert. The criteria evaluate the evidence and the evidence refines the criteria. But there must be a firm resolve to get the evidence, as far as is possible. If one begins here one is going by what I have called the inductive method.

This is in fact the method pursued by most work in moral theology today in all the main traditions which carry it on. If it is successful some general agreement emerges as to the facts of the situation, the main trends or tendencies at work, and the general direction or guidelines which Christian action should take. If there is no agreement then one cannot get as far as this and may only be able to point out the significant questions that need asking. This itself is valuable as far as it goes. The general direction is a middle level between basic values and aims and detailed policies. It has sometimes been called the level of middle axioms, a term adopted by Dr J. H. Oldham at the time of the formation of the World Council of Churches.[5] It is unlikely that agreement will reach as far as detailed policies, if only because they involve so many empirical details and forecasts about which there are inevitable uncertainties, that Christians committed to the basic aims may well disagree on the best way to implement them in detail. To decide this requires the traditional virtues of prudence and proportion. Once again we see that moral judgment is an art.

The study of Christian ethics and moral theology can certainly not be seen as an isolated discipline but is related to every other branch of theological study. The exegesis of the Bible is obviously involved, with all the problems of hermeneutics, that is, of understanding an ancient document in a modern cultural setting, which recent ecumenical studies have brought out. Doctrines of God as creator, redeemer and sanctifier, and therefore of man in relation to God and nature, are equally clearly involved. So is that of the church as the pilgrim body of Christ between the working out of the eschatological reality inaugurated in Jesus Christ and its future completion. The church as a subject of study involves an appreciation of the role of liturgy and worship, one aspect of which is to 'disinfect conduct from egoism'. The study of church history has a relativising effect as we take up any particular problem – be it usury, slavery, torture, religious liberty, contraception, property, anaesthetics, or the relieving of suffering, to name a few – and study it through the changing circumstances of the church. If it is an old problem we see how different the treatment has been, for instance, in the early church, in the Christendom situation, in the era of *laissez-faire* following the period of the Enlightenment, into the turbulent twentieth century of world wars, totalitarianism and the rise of protest against white hegemony and the influence of the 'Christian West'. The effect is to stress the concept of *ecclesia semper reformanda* in the field of ethics as well as doctrine, and in particular to undermine the ultramontane post-1870 tradition of moral theology in the Roman Catholic Church. Moreover, modern communications if nothing else have demonstrated that we live in one world and that in important respects we all stand or fall together. This has made the study of other religions (and total world views like Marxism) absolutely vital, and because of the increasingly pluralistic societies that are developing, new ways of relating to them. Further, it makes Christians take more seriously their doctrine of creation. It is clear that we are placed in basic structures, not by virtue of our Christian belief but by virtue of our common humanity. Moral theology must therefore show how distinctive Christian insights can contribute to the more just and humane working of the structures of life in which Christians and others live together. It must also foster as far as it can common insights with others on the basis of life together in a pluralist society. For society, except for a while by brutal totalitarian force, cannot be held together solely by law enforcement without some common convictions, which need clarifying and celebrating. Even prisons in the last resort can only continue with the goodwill of the prisoners. Marriage is another illustration of this. It is most important that Christians realize that they have a doctrine of marriage *as such*, not just of Christian marriage. In other words, marriage is primarily an order of creation. Realization of this has made Christians look much more carefully and positively at polygamy, and at African marriage in general, and in doing so useful insights into marriage as such have been gained.

Because Christians assume, with the Bible, that the human world is a moral world, that is to say a world where it is characteristic of man as man to make moral distinctions, and to know that what he considers right he ought to follow and what he considers wrong he ought to shun (even though he often does not do so), it is necessary for Christian ethics to pay attention to the work of the moral philosopher in illuminating the category of the moral. As always he will not do so uncritically. He will for instance think he has a better understanding of weakness of will in the moral life than is usually the case with moral philosophers. On the other hand, he has much to learn from moral philosophy in the exercise of moral reason and the formation of a sensitive conscience. Nor can he escape from unresolved dilemmas in moral philosophy, in particular the debate between deontological and teleological ethical theory. Like philosophy in general, moral philosophy is a sphere where issues go on being discussed, often for centuries, and get clarified by intense thought, but are not resolved and continually crop up again. The question of whether, or how far, particular moral issues can be resolved by following a rule independently of the consequences which result, or by estimating the likely consequence of possible actions in terms of an end aimed for, and choosing the one likely to maximize the good (however understood), is one such question. The proponents of each view put awkward questions to those of the other, and neither in the history of moral philosophy has ousted the other. A teleological or utilitarian approach has been dominant for some time, but there is some reaction against it lately in favour of a form of intuitionism and a concern for personal integrity as against consequentialism, but it is not clear how far it will get. Each side has at some time claimed that Christian ethics agrees with it. Kant thought it sided with him and J. S. Mill that it sided with him. In fact, it is not satisfied with either, but it cannot escape the dilemmas posed by both. Christians may talk of *agape*, or of an ethic of responsibility, but it does not avoid the problem of whether, or how far, in a particular case one decides by a rule derived from the Christian faith or by likely consequences evaluated in terms of criteria consonant with the Christian faith. I have my own ideas on this but this is not the occasion to elaborate them.

This is the chief issue involved in the situation ethics debate. It had been smouldering for a few years before Joseph Fletcher's book *Situation Ethics*[6] caused a furore, partly because of the lively, not to say swashbuckling, style in which it was written.

For a few more years the debate dominated the scene but it has died down lately. A survey of it should be written. My opinion is that the main point made by the proponents of situation ethics has been conceded, namely that the Christian life, or indeed human life, cannot be lived by fixed moral rules. Many of those who admit this tend to cover up the significance of doing so by at the same time passing adverse comments on situation ethics which is considered a theological *enfant terrible*. However, as we have seen, moral theology has come more and more to this point of view, and in certain moods it can say 'this is what was meant all along'. On the other hand it does not dispose of the awkward question of how a situation is to be defined and delineated. Nor does it dispose of the question of moral rules. After all life is not a series of extreme borderline situations which may require unusual and in some cases what would normally be considered shocking action. There is also personal and collective moral experience to be sifted and drawn upon. Moral wisdom does not arrive in an instant without father or mother. Discussion on these issues will continue, as the art of moral judgment is brought to bear with prudence and proportion on particular issues. There are also signs that attention is moving back rather more to questions of the general character and discrimination characteristic of Christian ethics, which is to the other half of the problem of the moral life. The work of Stanley Hauerwas, a Methodist who teaches at Notre Dame University, USA, is an instance of this. I refer to his *Vision and Virtue, Character and the Christian Life*, and *Truthfulness and Tragedy*.[7] His chief mentors appear to be Aristotle, Aquinas and the philosopher-novelist Iris Murdoch.

Roman Catholic moral theology has been able to take the situation ethics debate in its stride because nothing short of a revolution has taken place in it since the Second Vatican Council. However, all revolutions have precursors. Just as the vast liturgical changes initiated by the Council go back to the Liturgical Movement from the early years of this century, so the changes in moral theology go back to developments in the German school of moral theologians from the end of the nineteenth century. The upshot is that moral theology has become less formal, less legalistic, less essentialist, less tied to the confessional, and more scriptural, more humane and more concerned with norms arrived at from human experience. The teaching church has learned a lot from the experience of the laity in recent years.

III

I have given some account of where we are now and how we have got here, so I turn at last to venturing some reflections on where we may go in the next ten years. Perhaps the first question is, will there be a conservative backlash? There are signs of it. There is the phenomenon of the Festival of Light in Britain. Also there has clearly been a slowing up of the impetus to change in the Roman Catholic Church which Vatican II gave. I do not think the backlash will get very far. On the evangelical side there has been a break up of more monolithic positions in doctrine and ethics, so that there is now a spectrum of positions as within other Christian traditions. Some parts of the spectrum are shewing far more informed awareness of a far wider range of ethical issues than hitherto. Ten years ago we would not have found John Stott taking the chair for lectures delivered by the Latin American liberation theologian José Miguez Bonino on *Christians and Marxists*,[8] with the sub-title 'The Mutual Challenge to Revolution', and with a particularly warm reference by the author to his chairman in the preface. In the Roman Catholic Church it is very doubtful if the lid could be put back on all that came into the open after Vatican II, even if there were a desire to do it. Moreover the rapid social changes and the growth of pluralism will continue, so that it will be increasingly difficult for the churches to go back to their old methods unless they abandon all responsibility for society and take a sectarian 'Christ against Culture' attitude.

At the present the old and new tendencies exist side by side in the Roman Catholic Church. The Documents of Vatican II contain both, and the practice afterwards has exemplified both. In moral theology the encyclical *Populorum Progressio* of 1967 embodied the new, and *Humanae Vitae* in the next year the old. It is in questions of the ethics of sex that the old holds sway more than in others, and the recent *Declaration on Sexual Ethics* of the Congregation for the Doctrine of the Faith is another example. Both have had a rough reception. Will future teaching of the *magisterium* reflect the new or the old tendencies? Indeed will it be by encyclicals? It is noteworthy that when in 1971 the Pope wanted to commemorate the eightieth anniversary of the revival of Catholic social teaching in 1891 in Leo XIII's encyclical *Rerum Novarum* he did not write another encyclical, as had been done in 1931 with *Quadragesimo Anno* and in 1961 with *Mater et Magistra*, but sent a letter *Octogesima Adveniens* on the subject to Cardinal Roy, the President of the Pontifical Justice and Peace Commission.

It is questionable whether encyclicals are a good way for the church to produce her ethical teaching. Insofar as they attempt to relate to the modern world, is it adequate to produce documents which refer almost entirely to the early Fathers or previous Popes, or if they occasionally do give others references, to confine them to Roman Catholics and (with only a very few exceptions) theologians at that? It is frequently said one needs to know who drafts them. Unofficially this knowledge seems to creep out, and it is often disquieting. In the last analysis, however much authority the *magisterium* puts behind them they are going to stand or fall on their cogency. If they draw upon the thought of only a narrow range of experience or points of view they are not in the end going to carry weight. Once people begin to speculate about the drafters and their adequacy a good deal of the theorectical authority behind the encyclical is lost.

The documents of a Council like Vatican II are better in this respect. Much more is known about the process of discussion, drafting and re-drafting which lies behind them, and so are the names of the experts who were drawn into consultation. Even though these were largely ecclesiastical figures they ensured a diverse input, and the output in the shape of the Pastoral Constitution *Gaudium et Spes* was an impressive document of perception and humanity, which has provoked most of the forward looking work in moral theology in that field since the Council. *Humanae Vitae* on the other hand has led to defensive and inhibiting thought and action. In the case of comparable work in church and society in the World Council of Churches every detail in the process of reports is known. Drafts are circulated and criticized and re-drafted across the continents and across the confessions. Disagreements are open. Documents which arrive in the end carry a great deal of cogency if they are agreed, and where agreement proves impossible they are usually able to clarify the questions which are not agreed and indicate the further work needed.

Leaving population questions aside, the methods of Roman Catholic moral theology, of the World Council of Churches and of the various main confessional traditions, such as Lutheran, Anglican, Methodist, are becoming more and more alike. So it is not surprising that ever since the Second Vatican Council and the WCC Geneva Conference of 1966 the emphases of both bodies in the sphere of social ethics have been so similar. It has made possible the setting up under the joint sponsorship of the WCC and the Roman Catholic Justice and Peace Commission of SODEPAX (the Commission for Society, Development and Peace). It is no secret that the Vatican has been much more nervous of it than has the WCC because there are two tendencies, the new and the old, struggling within the Vatican. But it has survived and my guess is that it will continue.[9]

I say this because it is becoming clear that inter-confessional methodology in ethics allows different views to be expressed. The question has come up in the British context in connection with the refusal of the Roman Catholic hierarchy to become officially part of the British Council of Churches, although locally in Britain the Roman Catholic Church is often officially a member of local Councils of Churches. It had been expected to agree, and the main cause of its hesitation appeared to be nervousness as to whether it would be carried along by others in ethical stances with which the Roman Catholic Church does not agree. For instance, population questions have been a delicate matter ever since *Humanae Vitae*; and especially in the question of abortion. Roman Catholics have taken a much more thorough rule-based negative line than most Christians. A joint commission was appointed to look into this question. Its report, *Public Statements on Moral Issues*, was published in 1978 and concluded that the methodology of the British Council of Churches allows ethical differences between churches (and within) to be expressed, and there is no reason why Roman Catholics should not express themselves freely, so that if they have one position or a spectrum of positions (as is now often the case though not always admitted) there is no reason why they cannot be brought out and the grounds for them made clear.

It is to be hoped that more and more work in Christian ethics and moral theology will be done ecumenically, if only for the fact that if genuine dialogue and relevant expertise is involved in clarifying issues there are a limited number of experts whose goodwill can be called on. Also the greater the experience represented the greater weight the conclusions will carry. The onus would seem to be on those who wish to carry on in their confessional separation to justify themselves. I can think of no ethical problem which requires a confessional 'solution'. In this connection one must wonder whether it was wise for the English Roman Catholics recently to set up their own Linacre Centre for the study of health care. It is an imaginative project, a response to the rapidly growing problems of medical ethics which I have already mentioned. But it is hard to see what requires it to be a peculiarly Roman Catholic enterprise, except that it will cover some of the population questions where the *magisterium* has recently committed itself to the old way of doing moral theology.

In the next ten years in my judgment the process of 'indigenization' of moral theology will continue. By this I mean that wider experience will continue to be drawn on than in the past, which has been dominated by white, male, Western middle-class theologians. They have done some excellent work, which it is to be hoped will continue, but it clearly needs supplementing. More of the experience of non-Western churches needs drawing upon. We have seen that this is happening with respect to African marriage. It is happening, too, in the place which Latin American liberation theology has gained for itself since it first came to the attention of the rest of the world at the WCC Geneva Conference on Church and Society in 1966. True, the elements in it are almost entirely European in origin, but it reflects the Latin American situation. Or again women are being drawn into making their contribution on sexual ethics which has hitherto been the preserve of males, a majority of them celibates. Not much progress has been made in drawing working class experience into dialogue, except as mediated through middle class interpreters, but work put into urban and industrial mission is beginning to alter that.

For the rest I am pretty confident that the world will continue to provide the agenda, whether this is liked or not. Those who dislike it think that it means that the church capitulates to the latest modern fad and loses its distinctive message in trying to shew that it is up to date. That there is a danger of this no one can deny. But it is not inevitable if the reciprocal relationship is kept between an empirical investigation into what is going on and the criteria by which relevant facts are picked out and evaluated. Indeed there is no other way of proceeding which can avoid irrelevance. It is not a weakness to learn from and adapt to current experience, but a strength. A sociologist of religion like Bryan Wilson who, in his books *Religion and Secular Society*, and *Contemporary Transformations of Religion*,[10] interprets this as a disintegration of the Christian position completely misunderstands the nature of the Christian faith and ethic. The churches have come a long way in the last fifty or sixty years. Before that it is difficult to exaggerate how isolated they were from each other and how out of touch with what was actually going on. Now the situation is much improved. In particular it can be said with some confidence that their combined efforts have brought them up to date with the contemporary situation for the first time since the rapid social changes brought about by the Industrial Revolution began to have their world-wide impact; and for the first time since the break up of the Middle Ages they are able to have some small purchase over events, instead of trailing after them when it is too late. How far the opportunity is taken remains to be seen. But even to keep it open requires a continued, and indeed greater effort, for the speed of social change increases and becomes more global in its range. The churches have to work hard not to regress. To pause and stand still is not an option.

As to particular issues in moral theology which will dominate the next ten years, I can do no more, as I said at the beginning, than extrapolate from existing trends. The Western societies will be growingly preoccupied with problems of energy and affluence, together with the disappearance of unskilled jobs in industry and commerce. They were always dead-end jobs and there is no need to lament their disappearance. But in societies hitherto dominated by the remains of a Protestant work ethic it will not do to provide no work for a large element in the population. All human beings have personal qualities which need to be called on, because all human beings need to be wanted. We shall have greatly to expand the service element in our society by corporate provisions, at the same time as we realize that the competition for private goods on which our economic system has relied for motivation becomes self-defeating the more these private goods become accessible. Their attraction depended on their scarcity. Great changes in society will be called for which have hardly begun to be thought about. Another area of ethical decision which will be much to the fore is that of medicine, where the possibilities of 'genetical engineering' are beginning to outpace science fiction. As to the

Fourth (non-oil) World, I fear it will continue to be preoccupied with economic survival, and that the rest of the world – whether the First, Second or Third (oil) Worlds – will be tempted to live in a wealthy ghetto and largely ignore it. Further it is needless to say that problems of war, violence, crime and racialism will not go away.

However, it is not very fruitful to do more than give this brief indication of what the agenda is likely to be. Will the Christians and their churches shew better qualities of discernment in the next decade? Will they provide better guide lines? Will they ask more penetrating questions? Will they penetrate further into the likely secondary consequences of actions and policies when others are more short sighted? Will they overcome the perennial temptation to justify the *status quo* (often without realizing it is changing), or on the other hand to adopt utopian and over simplified stances which, when they fail, only lead to disillusionment? These are searching questions. In particular will the charismatic movement, which has certainly re-vivified the churches in some respects in recent years, produce greater discernment in ethical issues? With regret I have to say that I think not. My judgment at the moment is that in so far as the charismatic movement has spread from churches on the margins of society to middle class churches it has had the same effect as the Oxford Group (or Moral Re-armament) did forty years ago. It has broken down the reserve which characterizes so much middle class life and the worship of churches so much made up of middle class people. It has produced a much greater sense of corporateness which can only be welcomed. But in terms of social ethics it seems on the whole to lead to an evasion of responsibilities rather than a greater adequacy in meeting them.

In its task of training the quality of discernment the church is endeavouring to think and act with good judgment herself, and to produce men and women of good judgment. Good judgment is a matter of sensitivity drawing upon experience by rational reflection. It is a creative activity of the human moral reason, not rule based but one where rules have an important part to play. Apart from wrestling with the details of particular situations and issues there is the general task of looking out upon the world and arriving at adequate general insights to illuminate the details. From such insights will come the inspiration and perseverance needed to cope with the complex, long term, intractable and often potentially dangerous problems with which humanity has to live in the last fifth of the twentieth century. At this point we come to the possibilities of drawing from the Christian tradition, in reciprocal relation to our particpation in the web of human life, various images, parables, models, paradigms, ideologies and utopias. One or other of these terms is frequently quoted, usually in an imprecise way. A closer look at them, their nature, possibilities and potential dangers in Christian ethics and moral theology would be a fruitful use of the imagination. That, however, would require another essay.

Bibliography of Published Works

(contributions to books, and main articles, but only a very few reviews)

1936

'The World in the Church', *The Listener*, vol. XVI, 30 September, pp. 620–22

1937

'The Christian Case against Capitalism', *Radical Religion* (USA), Spring, vol. 2 no. 2, pp. 8–13

1938

'The Demand for Restatement' in *The Gospel to this Generation*, ed. M. H. Fitzgerald, Hodder & Stoughton 1938, pp. 132–38

1939

Christians in Society, with Edwin Barker, SCM Press 1939

1942

'The Malvern Conference', *The Modern Churchman*, vol. XXXII, April, pp. 15–22; reprinted as 'The Theology of the Malvern Conference' in *Radical Churchman* (USA), Summer

1943

'A Century of Anglican Social Thought', *The Modern Churchman*, vol. XXXII, January–March, pp. 337–47; reprinted in *Christianity and Society* (USA), Summer (the successor to *Radical Religion*)

1944

'Reinhold Niebuhr: Prophet and Philosopher', *The Modern Churchman*, vol. XXXIII, January–March, pp. 290–302

'The Religious and the Technical', *The Presbyter*, April, pp. 4–8

1946

'The Spring of Christendom' (review article on *Prospect for Christendom*, ed. M. B. Reckitt), *The Modern Churchman*, vol. XXXVI, June, pp. 15–24

'Britain and Labour Government', *Social Action* (USA), vol. XII no. 2, February, pp. 4–35

1947

'The Christian Student and his Studies', *Student World*, fourth quarter, pp. 325–35

1949

The Revelation of St John the Divine, Torch Bible Commentary, with Anthony Hanson, SCM Press 1949

1950

'Transfiguration', in *A Theological Word Book of the Bible*, ed. Alan Richardson, SCM Press 1950, pp. 267ff.

1953

'Later Books of the New Testament' in *Aids to the Teaching of Religious Knowledge*, Derbyshire County Education Committee, pp. 70–76

1954

'Is the University Question Dead?', *The Christian Scholar* (USA), June, vol. 37 no. 2, pp. 96–100

1955

'Revelation', *The Teachers' Commentary*, ed. G. Henton Davies and Alan Richardson, SCM Press 1955, pp. 513–18

Review of C. A. Pierce, *Conscience in the New Testament* (SCM Press), *Theology*, vol. 58, October, pp. 390–91

'The Political Situation in Britain: Autumn 1955', *Christianity and Crisis* (USA), 31 October, vol. XV no. 18, pp. 139–43

1959

'Christian Thinking in Britain on Social Ethics and Action', *Background Information for Church and Society*, WCC, March, no. 22, pp. 1–4

1960

'The Christian Left Still Lost', *Theology*, vol. 63, April, pp. 133–36
'Hesitations about the Parish Communion', *Theology*, vol. 63, September, pp. 365–69

1961

'Christian Ethics and Moral Theology 1939–60', *Theology*, vol. 64, part 1, January, pp. 3–7, part 2, February, pp. 46–57

1962

'Christianity, Religion and Political Radicalism', *Frontier*, vol. 5, Autumn, pp. 513–17

1964

'The Study of Christian Ethics', *Theology*, vol. 67, April, pp. 142–49
'Important Moral Issues – VI, Investment', *Expository Times*, vol. 75, June, pp. 275–79; reprinted under the same title in *Important Moral Issues*, ed. A. W. and E. Hastings, T. & T. Clark 1966

1965

'Worldly Holiness', *The Preachers' Quarterly*, December, pp. 301–5

1966

'Christians and Economic Growth', in *Economic Growth in World Perspective*, ed. Denys Munby (Geneva Conference Volume), SCM Press 1966, pp. 101–23; reprinted in *Die Kirche als Faktor einer Kommenden Weltgeimeinschaft*, Kreuz Verlag, Stuttgart 1966 and in *Contemporary Religion and Social Responsibility*, ed. N. Piediscalzí, Alba House, New York 1973
'R. H. Tawney as a Christian Moralist', *Theology*, vol. 69, April, May, June, pp. 157–64, 208–15 and 162–69; reprinted in *Religion and the Persistence of Capitalism*, SCM Press 1979
'The Kingdom of God in Economic Life' in *Politics and the Kingdom*, BBC Publications 1966
'The Presuppositions of Christian Theology' and 'Ethical Criticisms of Jesus', *Vindications*, ed. Anthony Hanson, SCM Press 1966, pp. 9–28 and 135–52; the second is reprinted in this volume

1967

Articles on: Artificial Insemination, Capital Punishment, Corporal Punishment, Compromise, Conscience, Vocation, Work, Welfare State,

Truth, Lying and False Witness in *A Dictionary of Christian Ethics*, ed. John Macquarrie, SCM Press 1967

'Christian Social Thinkers – Reinhold Niebuhr, *Crucible*, November, pp. 171–76

'The Ethical Claims of the Bible' in *The Bible Tells Me So*, ed. H. Loukes, BBC Publications 1967

1968

'I Recommend you to Read – XI, Recent Books on Christian Ethics', *Expository Times*, vol. 79, February, pp. 132–36

'The Sacred Ministry – 7: The Priest as a Teacher of Ethics in a Plural Society', *Theology*, vol. 71, July, pp. 305–10; reprinted in *The Sacred Ministry*, ed. G. R. Dunstan, SPCK 1970

1969

'Twenty Years of Teaching Christian Ethics', *Theology*, vol. 72, July, pp. 305–15

'William Temple: after Thirty-five Years', *Church Quarterly*, vol. 2, October, pp. 104–18

Review of *The Just War: Force and Political Responsibility*, Paul Ramsey in *Survival* (Institute of Strategic Studies), Autumn

1970

Articles on: Birth Control (Sterilization: Contraception) and Christian Ethics in *A Dictionary of Comparative Religion*, ed. S. G. F. Brandon, Weidenfeld and Nicholson 1970

'Human Freedom and Fulfilment in a World of Science-based Technology', *Study Encounter*, WCC, vol. 6 no. 2, pp. 55–65

1971

'A Breakthrough in Ecumenical Social Ethics?', in *Technology and Social Justice*, ed. R. H. Preston, SCM Press 1971; reprinted in this volume

'Middle Axioms in Christian Social Ethics, *Crucible*, January–February, pp. 9–15; reprinted in this volume

'On Teaching Christian Ethics: a Discussion Continued', *Theology*, vol. 74, December, pp. 577–82

1972

'On the Theological Fringe', *Expository Times*, vol. 83, March, pp. 168–72; reprinted in this volume

1974

'Ethical Aspects of Gambling: A New Look', *Crucible*, October–December, pp. 156–62

'Christians and Inflation', *One for Christian Renewal*, December

'Industrial Conflicts and the Dimensions of the Common Good', in *Industrial Conflicts and their Place in Modern Society*, ed. R. H. Preston, SCM Press 1974

'Das Wort der Kirche an die Wirtschaftgesellschaft' and 'Die Kirchen und das Wirtschaftsleben, (1) Der Wohfahrtsstaat und seine Zukunft (2) Arbeit und Industrie, (3) Der Reichtum und die Kirchen', in *Kirche und Wirtschaftsgesellschaft*, ed. W. Weber, Peter Haustein Verlag, Köln 1974

1975

'The Aims and Limits of the Consultation', in *Perspectives on Strikes*, ed. R. H. Preston, SCM Press 1975

'The Ethics of Investment', *Theology*, vol. 78, October, pp.

'Understanding the Unions', *Audenshaw Papers*, November

'Reflection on Theologies of Social Change', in *Theology and Change*, ed. (with introductory memoir of Alan Richardson) R. H. Preston, SCM Press 1975; reprinted in *Religion and the Persistence of Capitalism*, SCM Press 1979

1976

'The Education of Clergy and Ministers', in *Education for the Professions*, ed. John D. Turner and James Rushton, Manchester University Press 1976, pp. 38–51

'From the Bible to the Modern World: A Problem in Ecumenical Ethics', *Bulletin of the John Rylands Library*, vol. 59 no. 1, Autumn, pp. 164–87; reprinted in this volume

'Introduction: Thirty-five Years Later 1941–76', introduction to the re-issue of William Temple, *Christianity and Social Order*, SPCK and Shepheard-Walwyn 1976; reprinted in this volume

Foreword memoir to the reissue of R. E. C. Browne, *The Ministry of the Word*, SCM Press 1976

1977

'Church and Class' review of E. R. Norman, *Church and Society in England 1770–1970*, Oxford University Press 1976, *The Modern Churchman*, new series vol. XX no. 3, pp. 84–94; reprinted in this volume

'Conscience and Inflation', *Acta Monetaria*, no. 1 (Frankfurt am Main), pp. 31–44

'Secularization and Renewal', *Crucible*, April–June, pp. 68–76

1978

'Whither Social Ethics?', *The Modern Churchman*, new series vol. XXI nos. 2–3, pp. 81–95; reprinted under the title 'The Scene in Christian Social Ethics' in *Religion and the Persistence of Capitalism*, SCM Press 1979

'The Depositing of Cultural and Artistic Objects in Banks: Some Ethical Observations', *Acta Monetaria*, no. 2 (Frankfurt am Main)

'Anglican and Ecumenical Styles in Social Ethics', *Crucible*, July–September, pp. 117–126; reprinted in this volume

1979

'Need Dr Nineham be so Negative?', *Expository Times*, vol. 90, June, pp. 275–80

Religion and the Persistence of Capitalism (The Maurice Lectures for 1977), SCM Press 1979

1980

'The Next Ten Years in Christian Ethics and Moral Theology', in *Imagination and the Future*, ed. J. A. Henley, Hawthorn Press, Melbourne 1980; reprinted in this volume

'Towards Transnational Social Ethics?', in *Churches and Transnational Enterprises: Dialogues in Europe* 1975–80, UNIAPAC, Brussels; reprinted in this volume

'Social Theology and Penal Theory and Practice: the Collapse of the Rehabilitative Ideal and the Search for an Alternative', *The Coming Penal Crisis*, ed. A. E. Bottoms and R. H. Preston, Scottish Academic Press 1980, pp. 109–25

'The Question of a Just, Participatory and Sustainable Society', *Bulletin of the John Rylands Library*, vol. 63 no. 1, Autumn, pp. 95–117

Review of *Faith and Science in an Unjust World*, vol. 1 Plenary Presentations, ed. Roger Schinn, vol. 2 Reports and Recommendations, ed. Paul Abrecht (volumes arising out of the WCC Conference on 'Faith, Science and the Future' 1979), *The Ecumenical Review*, vol. 32 no. 4, October, pp. 456–58

'Understanding Resurrection Faith', in *The Modern Churchman*, new series vol. XXIII no. 2, Summer

1981

'Not Out of the Wood Yet: a Recent Christian Socialist Manifesto', *Theology*, vol. 84, March, pp. 83–87

'The Faculty of Theology in the University of Manchester: the First Seventy-five Years', *Bulletin of the John Rylands Library*, vol. 63 no. 2 Spring

Notes

1. Ethical Criticisms of Jesus

Originally published in *Vindications*, ed. Anthony Hanson, SCM Press 1966, pp. 136–52

1. Cf. 'The Presuppositions of Christian Theology' in *Vindications*, ed. Anthony Hanson, SCM Press 1966, ch. 1, pp. 9ff.

2. See H. W. Montefiore, *Awkward Questions on Love*, Collins 1964.

3. C. G. Montefiore, *Rabbinic Literature and Gospel Teachings*, Macmillan 1930, p. 104.

4. Cf. H.-G. Koch, *The Abolition of God*, SCM Press 1963.

5. Richard Robinson, *An Atheist's Values*, Oxford University Press 1964, pp. 140–55.

6. 'No belief is as such morally wrong; but it is morally wrong to form one's beliefs in view of something other than truth and probability; and Jesus demanded this moral wrong. It is a moral wrong whose harmful and degrading effects penetrate widely and are great. It is terrible to think how many million people have, as a result of those passages in the Gospels about having faith, done what probably each one of us here did in his childhood, tried to hypnotize himself into some particular belief and to disregard whatever scraps of judgment he possessed. The fine things in Jesus' teaching have been and will be greatly harmed by this blasphemy against reason', Robinson, op. cit., p. 151.

7. Some people have found no sense of humour in Jesus and regarded this as a moral defect in that to possess such a sense is a sign that we do not take ourselves too seriously. But humour is concerned with the penultimate not the ultimate things of life (to borrow terms from Bonhoeffer's *Ethics* (ET 2nd rearranged edition, SCM Press 1971), and Jesus concentrates on the ultimate. At this level humour is swallowed up in joy, and there is much evidence in all the gospels of Jesus' joy. To enquire what effect this joy had on his facial muscles would be pedantic.

8. The Shema (Deut. 6.4 and 11.13) from which Jesus was quoting has 'heart', and in the Septuagint *dianoia* often translates the Hebrew for heart; but as 'heart' is also in the Lord's summary it is possible that the insertion of 'mind' as well may be no more than a doublet.

9. Matt. 5.32, etc., discussed in all standard books and commentaries.

10. I Corinthians is particularly illuminating in this connection.

11. It developed points he had previously made in *The Rationalist Annual* in 1961 in an article 'Morality – Religious and Secular', reprinted in *Christian Ethics and Contemporary Philosophy*, ed. Ian T. Ramsey, SCM Press 1966, pp. 95–112.

12. A similar charge was made by John Elsom in a radio programme in January 1962. He maintained that Christianity, because of its moral authoritarianism, hampers the growth of moral awareness. It encourages stock moral reactions applied without regard to particular facts, and prevents us from learning from experience; so the growth of moral awareness is blocked and we are not helped to face situations objectively and to meet them.

2. A Breakthrough in Ecumenical Ethics?

Originally published in *Technology and Social Justice*, ed. R. H. Preston, SCM Press 1971, pp. 15–40. The second section of the original article entitled 'The Background and Structure of the Symposium' has been omitted.

1. See also the article by A. Schmémann in the original symposium – 'Theology or Ideology?', *Technology and Social Justice*, ch. 11, pp. 226ff.

2. *Christian Social Ethics in a Changing World*, ed. J. C. Bennett; *Economic Growth in World Perspective*, ed. D. Munby; *Responsible Government in a Revolutionary Age*, ed. Z. K. Matthews; *Man in Community*, ed. E. de Vries (all published by SCM Press 1966). Many of the essays were issued in German in one volume, *Die Kirche als Faktor einer kommenden Weltgemeinschaft*, Kreuz-Verlag, Stuttgart 1966.

3. Details in *Study Encounter* (WCC), vol. II, no. 2, 1966.

4. In 1967 Pope Paul's encyclical *Populorum Progressio* followed the general lines of the Geneva Conference and just as radically.

5. Report in *Study Encounter*, vol. IV, no. 2, 1968.

6. A further expert conference on 'The Challenge of Development', which took the Beirut material further, was held at Montreal in May 1969, and one on 'Theological Issues of Development' in November 1969 in Switzerland.

7. It is proper to mention here the work of guiding that Department undertaken by the Rev. Paul Abrecht for over twenty years. To him more than any other single person is due the Geneva Conference and all that preceded and has followed it.

8. In a personal comment on the work of Section III at Uppsala, Chief Justice Cowan of Nova Scotia refers to pressures on sections and sub-sections to produce a draft report at an early stage of their work. He points out the importance of adequate time, especially for those not fluent in one of the major languages used to speak their minds, and pleads for 'more time for section members to read and digest the material placed before them and to discuss intelligently the issues

raised', *Uppsala 68 Speaks: The Message and Section Reports of the Assembly*, WCC 1968, p. 56.

9. Paul Ramsey, *Who Speaks for the Church?*, Abingdon Press, USA 1967, a Methodist publishing house; in 1969 it was published in Britain by the St Andrew Press, a Church of Scotland one. Ramsey presumably sees no need to modify it since 1967.

10. The British delegates, for instance, none of whom as far as I am aware were in favour of Ian Smith's regime, found themselves having to fight very hard in the full Assembly to modify an ill-informed resolution addressed to the British Government, to make it adequate. In the circumstances proper discussion was impossible. The passing of such resolutions was not the job of the Conference.

11. Ramsey, op. cit., p. 77.

12. *Christians in the Technical and Social Revolution of Our Time*, WCC 1967: the Report of the World Conference on Church and Society held at Geneva, July 1966, pp. 203f.

13. A splendid example from an earlier epoch is one of the Archbishop's Peace Points in war-time Britain: 'The real needs and just demands of nations should be benevolently examined.'

14. But things may get to a desperate pass in countries where the church has had no power or opportunity to prevent it, and where the church (unless totally silenced) is driven to specific positions perforce. In short, a 'gates of Auschwitz' situation may arise more often than those living in relatively stable constitutional democracies think.

15. Ramsey, op. cit., p. 119.

16. Ibid., pp. 135f.

17. See e.g. *The Church and its Function in Society*, ed. J. H. Oldham and W. A. Visser't Hooft, Allen & Unwin 1937 (for the Oxford Conference see p. 210); and *Man's Disorder and God's Design*, vol. 3, *The Church and the Disorder of Society*, SCM Press 1948 (for the Amsterdam Assembly see note on p. 28).

18. The Christian as a citizen is, of course, required to go further in detailed political judgments if he lives in a state where there is scope for political participation, and sources of information. Ramsey is prone to make too wide a gulf between the 'magistrates' who have the duty of making political and public decisions and those in whose name and on whose behalf they do it. There have been enough blunders made by elected representatives and their expert advisers in the recent history of the West (to look no further) to make unconvincing a sharp division between those who are competent to speak on policy matters and those who are not.

19. Paul Ramsey, *The Just War*, Scribners, New York 1968, p. 457; *Who Speaks for the Church?*, p. 140.

3. *Middle Axioms in Christian Social Ethics*
Originally published in *Crucible*, January–February 1971,
pp. 9–15.

1. Paul Ramsey, *Who Speaks for the Church?*, St Andrew Press 1969.
2. J. H. Oldham and W. A. Visser't Hooft (eds), *The Church and its Function in Society*, Allen & Unwin 1937.
3. John Bennett, *Christian Social Action*, Lutterworth 1954.
4. Reinhold Niebuhr, 'God's Design and the Present Disorder of Society', *The Church and the Disorder of Society*, SCM Press 1948, p. 28 note 1.

4. *On the Theological Fringe*
Originally published in *The Expository Times*, Vol. 83, March 1972,
pp. 168–71.

1. The Samuel Ferguson Chair in Social and Pastoral Theology was established by the University of Manchester in 1970, having been endowed by the Samuel Ferguson Trustees. Ferguson was a Manchester man who developed the Ferguson Pailin Switchgear (now part of AEI). A devout Methodist, he left one third of his estate to the Trust which he had established before his death. Manchester does not have the custom of inaugural lectures by newly elected Professors, but in this case the student Theological Society invited the Professor to explain himself and suggested his title. This is a shortened version of what I said.
2. Paul Tillich, *On the Boundary: An Autobiographical Sketch*, with an introduction by J. Heywood Thomas, Collins 1967.
3. H. Thielicke, *The Ethics of Sex*, James Clarke 1967, p. 199 (a section of his *Theological Ethics* issued separately in English).
4. H. E. Root, 'Beginning All Over Again', *Soundings*, Cambridge University Press 1966, pp. 1–19.
5. See Ch. 3 above.

5. *From the Bible to the Modern World*
Originally published in *Bulletin of the John Rylands Library*, Vol.
59, no. 1, Autumn 1976, pp. 164–87.

1. Richard Niebuhr, *Christ and Culture*, Harper & Row 1951.
2. Alan Richardson and Wolfgang Schweitzer (eds), *Biblical Authority for Today*, SCM Press 1951.
3. Richardson and Schweitzer, op. cit., pp. 240ff.
4. Ibid., p. 241.
5. Ibid., p. 242.
6. Ibid., p. 243.
7. *The Fourth World Conference on Faith and Order*, ed. P. C. Rodger and L. Vischer, Montreal 1963; *New Directions in Faith and Order*, Bristol 1967; *Faith and Order*, Louvain 1971.

8. E. Flesseman-van Leer, 'Biblical Interpretation in the World Council of Churches', *Study Encounter*, vol. 8, no. 2, 1972.

9. Albert Schweitzer, *The Quest of the Historical Jesus*, ET third edition, A. & C. Black 1954, reissued SCM Press 1981, p. 397.

10. Leonard Hodgson, *For Faith and Freedom*, SCM Press 1968 edition, preface, pp. xff.

11. E. Flesseman-van Leer, op. cit.

12. I would go further and say that the church will not go fundamentally astray in her reflection on the witness of the Bible to the centrality of Jesus Christ; that is to say that she will in time correct her own distortions. I think there is much cogency in this respect in Hans Küng's treatment of indefectibility in his book *Infallible?* (Collins 1971), but this is another presupposition which cannot be developed now.

13. There is a useful and brief appendix 'Note on the Use of the Bible' in *Teaching Christian Ethics*, sponsored by the Advisory Council for the Church's Ministry of the Church of England, SCM Press 1974.

14. E. Käsemann, 'The Beginnings of Christian Theology', *New Testament Questions of Today*, SCM Press 1969, pp. 82–107.

15. Kenneth Kirk, *The Vision of God*, Longmans Green 1931.

16. Thomas Aquinas, *Summa Theologiae* 2a. 2ae q.XL arts 1–4.

17. Jack T. Sanders, *Ethics in the New Testament*, SCM Press 1975.

18. Käsemann, op. cit., p. 108.

19. W. Pannenberg, *Basic Questions in Theology*, SCM Press 1970, chs 1 and 2; J. Moltmann, *Theology of Hope*, SCM Press 1967, ch. 2; and Moltmann, *The Experiment Hope*, SCM Press 1975, ch. 4.

20. Most of this is quoted from an essay of mine 'Reflections on Theologies of Change' pp. 156f., in R. H. Preston (ed.), *Theology and Change*, SCM Press 1975. It is interesting to note that Martin Buber takes the same adverse view of apocalyptic (as compared with prophecy) in *Pointing the Way*, ET Routledge 1957, pp. 192–207. Because the future is destined, the present loses its value, and faithful endurance is all that can be called for from the individual. Cf. also Sophie Laws, 'Can Apocalyptic be Relevant?' in *What about the New Testament?*, ed. Morna Hooker and Colin Hickling, SCM Press 1975.

21. E.g. Fletcher, *Situation Ethics*, SCM Press 1966; *Moral Responsibility*, SCM Press 1967; A. Nygren, *Agape and Eros*, revised ET, SPCK 1953.

22. Karl Barth, *Christengemeinde und Bürgergemeinde*, 1946, ET 'The Christian Community and the Civil Community' in *Against the Stream*, SCM Press 1954, §22.

23. Karl Barth, *Church Dogmatics*, ET T. & T. Clark 1961, especially III/1, §41.

6. *Thirty-five Years Later, 1941–76 – William Temple's* Christianity and Social Order

Originally published as the introduction to the reissue of William Temple, *Christianity and Social Order*, SPCK and Shepheard-Walwyn 1976.

1. Denys Munby, *God and the Rich Society*, Oxford University Press 1960.

2. But note his Beckley Social Service Lecture 1943 – 'Social Witness and Evangelism'.

3. See Ch. 3 above.

4. R. H. Tawney, *Religion and the Rise of Capitalism*, John Murray 1926, Penguin Books 1938; Charles Gore (ed.), *Property: its Duties and Rights*, Macmillan 1913.

5. F. A. Iremonger, *William Temple*, Oxford University Press 1948, p. 438.

6. J. S. Carmichael and H. S. Goodwin, *William Temple's Political Legacy*, Mowbray 1963.

7. Robert Craig, *Social Concern in the Thought of William Temple*, Gollancz 1963.

8. A. M. Ramsey, *From Gore to Temple*, Longmans 1960.

9. Richard Niebuhr, *Christ and Culture*, Harper and Row 1951.

10. J. H. Oldham and W. A. Visser't Hooft (eds), *The Church and its Function in Society*, Allen & Unwin 1937.

11. A. P. d'Entrèves, *Natural Law*, Hutchinson 1951.

12. This is constantly being pointed out. An exposition in a contemporary context is that of the distinguished Harvard economist J. K. Galbraith, who writes so readably that he can command Pelican editions of his books. His *Economics and the Public Purpose*, Deutch 1974, Penguin Books 1975.

13. John Macmurray, *The Self as Agent*, Faber 1957; *Persons in Relation*, Faber 1961; *Freedom in the Modern World*, Faber 1932.

14. *Quadragesimo Anno*, 1931, §80.

15. A. D. Lindsay, *The Essentials of Democracy*, OUP 1929; *The Churches and Democracy*, Epworth Press 1934.

16. See Ch. 2 above.

17. *Christianity and Society*, vol. 8, no. 3, 1943. I am reminded of this – for I was in fact the British agent for the journal at the time – by a research student of mine, Mr J. R. Atherton of the William Temple Foundation, to whom I am much indebted for the reference to Buonauti, and for discussing this introduction with me in the light of two unpublished papers by him, 'William Temple and Politics', and 'The Reconstruction of the British Christian Social Tradition'.

18. José Miguez Bonino, *Revolutionary Theology Comes of Age*, SPCK 1975.

19. Certainly it is not possible to put *order* so unequivocally as the first political requisite as Temple does (p. 61), because we have become much more conscious of the 'established disorder' of many political

systems, and of the 'institutional violence' expressed in many ostensibly powerful structures.

20. *The Economic Review*, 1908, vol. XVIII, p. 199.

21. Many Christians have not seen this, and adopt an individualistic ethic partly because it is not the focus of the teaching of Jesus, nor was it the focus of the early church with its belief in the imminent *parousia* and its insignificant position in the Roman Empire. Temple brings the question of the role of groups to the forefront, though he could have spelt out more fully how he related it theologically to his fundamental stress on the status of person.

22. Paul Ramsey, *Who Speaks for the Church?*, St Andrew Press 1967.

7. Anglican and Ecumenical Styles in Social Ethics
Originally published in *Crucible*, July–September 1978, pp. 117–126

1. Kenneth Kirk, *Conscience and Its Problems*, Longmans 1927.
2. Brian Barry, *The Liberal Theory of Justice*, Clarendon 1973.
3. John Rawls, *A Theory of Justice*, Oxford University Press 1972.

8. From Oxford to Nairobi
1. The Roman Catholic Church is officially part of the Faith and Order side of the WCC.
2. The title of the conference was in fact 'Faith, Science and the Future'; its plenary presentations and its reports and recommendations are respectively available in two books published by the WCC in 1980 under the title *Faith and Science in an Unjust World*, vol. 1, ed. Roger Shinn; vol. 2 ed. Paul Abrecht.

10. Church and Class
Originally published in *The Modern Churchman*, New Series vol. XX no. 3, Spring 1977, pp. 84–94

1. E. R. Norman, *Church and Society in England 1770–1970*, Oxford University Press 1976; the price was £15.

11. Towards Transnational Social Ethics?
Originally written for a Churches-Transnational Corporation symposium, organized by the International Christian Union of Business Executives (UNIAPAC) 49, avenue d'Auderghem, 1040 Brussels, in May 1979. Reprinted from 'Churches-Transnational Corporations European Dialogues, 1975–80', Business for People series 2/1980.

12. The Next Ten Years in Christian Ethics and Moral Theology
Originally published in *Imagination and the Future*, ed. J. A. Henley, Hawthorn Press, Melbourne 1980, pp. 253–71

1. H. Kahn and A. J. Weiner, *The Year 2000*, Macmillan 1967.

2. A. Nygren, *Agape and Eros*, ET revised ed., SPCK 1953.

3. Kenneth Kirk, *The Vision of God*, Longmans Green 1931.

4. G. Outka and P. Ramsey (eds), *Norm and Context in Christian Ethics*, SCM Press 1969.

5. See Ch. 3 above.

6. Joseph Fletcher, *Situation Ethics*, SCM Press 1966.

7. Stanley Hauerwas, *Vision and Virtue*, Fides, Indiana 1974; *Character and the Christian Life*, Trinity University Press 1975; *Truthfulness and Tragedy*, with Richard Bondi and David B. Burrell, University of Notre Dame Press 1977.

8. José Miguez Bonino, *Christians and Marxists*, Hodder & Stoughton 1976.

9. I was wrong: SODEPAX was discontinued at the end of 1980.

10. Bryan Wilson, *Religion and Secular Society*, Penguin Books 1966; *Contemporary Transformations of Religion*, Oxford University Press 1976.

Index